Ivor Ballott is the latest in a string of a score or more *nom de plumes* to be adopted by the writer Ian Shingler.

Born in London in 1948, Ian showed some writing skills in his youth. He wrote his first full-length play at the age of ten, won his first poetry prize at the age of eleven, and began having his prose published in his early teens.

In 1970 he co-founded the Hertfordshire Poets and Writers Circle which rapidly grew into a thriving group of around sixty members. At the same time, Ian founded his own publishing company, which enabled almost all of them to have work published or performed on stage or TV.

In the early 1970s, Ian was the group's most prolific writer, with over 400 poems published world-wide, as well as prose and plays. Much of it used a variety of pseudonyms.

President of the International Poetry Society from 1972-1974, he retired from full-time writing on his marriage in 1974, to concentrate on a commercial print career.

For the remainder of the 1970s and much of the 1980s, his small output concentrated on military history, mostly published in specialist journals.

After an active life as resident's leader, school governor etc, he was persuaded to stand for his local District Council in 1988, and captured the seat with a landslide victory.

Full-time employment and an active life as a Councillor resulted in a further reduction in time available for writing. However, he became one of the principle writers of political leaflets for his local party, as well as the very occasional magazine article on other subjects.

However, the lure of the pen to write something more substantial, and the challenge of writing for a wider audience, remained. As a result he has written 'The Chamber of Horrors', his second novel.

Ian lives in a Bedfordshire village with his wife Gabrielle. They have two daughters.

Matt Willis is one of Britain's finest up and coming artists linked to Mid Beds Art Society.

For as long as he can remember, he has always had a love of drawing. His drawings have always entertained because of their amusing content.

Whilst looking forward to a career in acting, he compliments this with his art work, of which 'Chamber Of Horrors' is his latest project.

He lives in a bedfordshire village.

THE CHAMBER
OF HORRORS

Ivor Ballott

The Chamber
of Horrors

Illustrated by Matt Willis

Vanguard Press

VANGUARD PAPERBACK

© Copyright 2004
Ivor Ballott

A CIP catalogue record for this title is
available from the British Library
ISBN 1 843860 80 5

*Vanguard Press is an imprint of
Pegasus Elliot MacKenzie Publishers Ltd.*
www.pegasuspublishers.com

First Published in 2004

**Vanguard Press
Sheraton House Castle Park
Cambridge England**

Printed & Bound in Great Britain

Dedication

This book is dedicated to

Maggie

Whose policies I detested so much that I became
involved in local politics.

And to

Gabrielle

Who has had to bear the brunt of my political
ranting and raving ever since.

AUTHOR'S PREFACE

I came into politics by chance, having been one of those 'committee-type' people who was always involved in organising something or other, instead of just sensibly taking part and enjoying myself, like everyone else.

In one of his books, the criminologist Colin Wilson goes through a gradual procession of what drives people to commit certain types of crime. Starting with the basic needs such as food and shelter, he progresses through sex crime, and postulates that mankind is now entering a new era: the point at which people commit crime for reasons of 'prestige'.

By this, he means crimes whose sole purpose seems to be to get noticed: the fifteen minutes of fame that we are all supposed to crave. The apparently pointless mass-shootings, notably in America, have happened since he published his theories, and appear to prove him right.

But Wilson's theory is just as relevant for the law-abiding citizen. Having acquired the essentials of life: a semi-detached rabbit hutch with an attached mortgage; sufficient nourishment for my waistline to be forever expanding; and a quantity of sexual gratification (show me any normal man who claims enough, and I'll introduce you to a liar), had brought me to the 'prestige' point.

No surprise then, that persuading me to run for the local council was easy: like most people, my ego loves being nurtured with enthusiastic praise, however unwarranted.

Once elected, I was determined to retain two things.

The first was common sense, a commodity, alas, in short supply with too many of 'the great and the good' of local politics. It isn't that they don't mean well; good intentions remain the prime aspiration of almost all of them. It's just that it is terribly easy to be sucked into "this is how it's always done" syndrome, however daft the likely outcome.

The second was to retain my wicked, even perverse, sense of humour. Sarcasm may be the lowest form of wit, but it's still terrific for deflating self-opinionated windbags, (as a councillor, a club of which I am now a fully paid-up member). The scenes and characters in this book are all fictitious, apart from a few figures of National notoriety brought in to add an element of historical context and background information. Perhaps it would be more accurate to call them factitious. That is to say that incidents are often a complete retelling of an actual event, while the personnel that inhabit the stories can be likened to a pack of cards. In real life each person is given a hand of cards. I have taken the cards away, given them a good shuffle, and redealt them to the characters in the book.

Doubtless my many colleagues on the council will recognise those flawed individuals as other councillors, whilst identifying themselves with the few heroic acts in the book.

IVOR BALLOTT (aka Councillor Ian Shingler)

PROLOGUE

It is towards the end of the 1980s.

Queen Maggie the Vindictive rules her domain with an iron rod, striking down ally and foe alike if they stand in her way.

Her enemies are scattered to the four winds.

She has utterly devastated the plebeians' economic powerbase, by systematically destroying the nation's manufacturing industry and thereby depriving them of their 'tithes'.

The moderates are in utter disunity, being unable even to pick their own leader, let alone one for the country.

The urban peasants are dispersed.

Some have been driven to the desolate wastelands of unemployment, there to eke out a wretched existence for the rest of their curtailed lives.

Others have erroneously convinced themselves that they are now members of the middle classes, and slavishly follow "the Word according to Maggie".

Her divided enemies clump together in small groups, each becoming smaller, weaker and more obscure with the passing years.

Meanwhile, in the nondescript village of Oakleigh, John Edwards lives quietly with his family, unaware of his destiny and the infinitesimal part he is eventually to play in the overthrow of Mag the Hag.

Armed only with the Sword of Good Intent and the Shield of Common Sense, he is about to embark unwittingly on a battle against Queen Maggie's hordes.

This will see him rise from total obscurity to almost total obscurity in a vicious fight to the electoral death in the famous Jousting Tournament of the Local Election Ballot Box.

This first volume in John's story tells the tale of how he is recruited by the self-proclaimed Forces of Good, and how he successfully begins to unravel his beloved nation from Maggie's Web of Evil.

Well, that's my version of events anyway.

Editor's note for younger readers:

Queen Maggie, the Vindictive and Mag the Hag, are nick-names for Margaret Thatcher, British Prime Minister 1979-1990.

Part One

The
Irresistible Rise of ME

CHAPTER ONE

THAT BLASTED OAK

We had only recently moved from the urban sprawl of Grimchester to the nearby village of Oakleigh, when in one of those quirks of Fate, I was plunged into that murky unseen world known as local politics.

The village numbers a mere 2,000 souls and its sleepy facade hides what would once have been considered a town, just as Grimchester is now a city, in all but name.

Oakleigh is perhaps the sleepiest corner of Sleepyvale District Council, a village quite unremarkable apart from its solitary claim to fame – King Henry's Oak Tree.

According to legend (or history, if you believe in the story), King Henry VIII stayed in Oakleigh in the early part of the sixteenth-century during a Progress around the country. These Progresses were a regular feature of six-teenth century life, the Tudor equivalent of the kind of tour nowadays organised by Wallace Arnold and somesuch. The Royal entourage even went from place to place in the most luxurious coaches money could buy.

However, they served an entirely different purpose to sightseeing, giving the servants left behind the ecstatic pleas-ure of scraping off the worst of the filth from the Kings homes while he was away. Had the expression 'getting away from it all' been in vogue at the time, doubtless the getting away would have been from picturesque dwellings with no sanitation and no dustmen to take away the rubbish.

An encounter with a swine.

Anyway, according to the story, King Henry stayed overnight at a tavern in Oakleigh. On the morrow (the next day to you or me), he was introduced to the local yeoman farmers, one of whom had a prize pig. The youthful King, who would himself one day resemble the prize sow, was so impressed that he took to feeding it acorns with his own royal hands.

After King Henry left, the sow apparently succumbed to acute diarrhoea, and from the largest pile of pig shit, there sprang overnight an oak sapling, henceforth to be known as King Henry's Oak, and now the principle tourist attraction of the village of Oakleigh. The tree stood alone, though not forgotten, in a small green field on the edge of the village.

We had not long moved into our new home in Regis Gardens, behind the Royal Oak public house, and only a few minutes walk from the famous tree. I was sitting down to breakfast reading the Clarion, Sleepyvale's weekly contribution to literature and investigative journalism, and like other local readers was stunned by the front page news:

KING HENRY'S OAK
TO BE FELLED
FOR NEW HOUSING ESTATE

This was outrageous – here was our very heritage being destroyed for a few more houses that the village neither needed nor wanted. (Like most of the other residents, we had moved the ten miles from Grimchester specifically to escape from the herds of new housing estates that were grazing the formerly verdant fields there. Once settled, we didn't want those same herds migrating to Oakleigh.)

The details of the story were sketchy – a major house-building company had applied to build seventeen houses on the field containing King Henry's Oak, and in the process, the tree would have to go. Seventeen houses on a field so small, the idea staggered belief – surely if you put a slide and two swings next to the tree, the field would be full up.

My wife, Penny, seemed unperturbed by the news. All she said was: "Well it looks just about ready to fall down anyway," and then resumed her attack on the toast and marmalade.

Never one to sit back complaining without doing anything, I resolved to see what we could do about saving the tree. After all, the British Empire was built on the oaks of England.

That evening, being a Friday, was my traditional night out at the pub with the lads. I have never much cared for the Royal Oak. Whether it had any association with the tale of King Henry, I cannot tell. Certainly its cobwebs could have been around since Tudor times. The other pub in the village, the Pig and Crown, was far more welcoming.

The first couple of pints were spent discussing a more important event: football, the usual dismal performance of Grimchester United on the previous Saturday and their likelihood of surviving in the Football League.

Of course, if only the club manager would listen to us experts about who to play, and in what formation, then Grimchester would be fighting its way towards the First Division instead of staring towards the Conference League, and beyond that the senior division of Scrummy Biscuits West Anglian League.

By the third pint, our talk had turned to King Henry's Oak, or at least mine had; my mates, Jim and Greg, were far too busy in a verbal sparring match as to which of them could pull the new barmaid.

After grudgingly learning the facts, Jim suggested that we ought to start a petition to save the tree, and that started the ball rolling. The fight to save our oak tree was now on, and we rolled up our sleeves ready for the fight.

By the following week, we had written, photocopied and delivered leaflets to most of the houses in the village, leaving out only those with unreasonably long drives, and a few outlying farms.

DON'T LET THEM BULLDOZE DOWN
KING HENRY'S OAK
COME TO A PROTEST MEETING
AT THE VILLAGE HALL
NEXT TUESDAY AT 8 P.M.
(13TH JANUARY)
SIGN OUR PETITION
AND
SAVE OAKLEIGH'S HERITAGE

The turnout for the meeting was impressive. By 7.45 p.m., around thirty people had drifted in. Unfortunately, in addition to the provisional acting committee (Jim, Greg and myself), this had declined to just eight fifteen minutes later, when our 'audience' realised that the Annual General Meeting of Oakleigh Allotments Association was being held in an adjacent room, where a crucial vote on allotment rents was due to take place.

Nevertheless we were undismayed and, with a simple show of hands, the grandiose sounding Oakleigh Tree Conservation and Heritage Preservation Group came into being

Greg then nominated me as chairman, because I had a word processor and printer at home, as well as a basic grasp of spelling and grammar, and a show of relieved hands confirmed the appointment, most of the small gathering being grateful to have escaped too active an involvement in the campaign.

The following day, bolstered by my new position, I telephoned the Planning Department of Sleepyvale District Council, asking how to register the group's objections to the plan to chop down King Henry's Oak for houses. A helpful lady came to the telephone and skilfully juggled the attribute of being very patient with that of absolute boredom at being asked a similar question yet again.

She explained that it was two days to late to object, and that the developers had already been given outline permission under delegated powers, which meant that it wouldn't even be discussed by the Planning Committee. I didn't understand what she was talking about, although it didn't take a genius to work out that it sounded as if we were too late.

She went on to inform me that the field had been ear-marked for development in the local plans published some years earlier. The plans had gone out for 'public consulta-tion', and any objections at the time would have been taken into consideration by the planning committee that ap-proved the plans.

"So members of the public were consulted at that time about demolishing the tree and building houses? The Council went out and spoke to local residents?" I asked na-ively.

"Oh no, nothing like that," she replied, with a com-bined expression of amusement and annoyance at my ob-vious ignorance. "When we talk about public consultation, we mean leaving copies of the draft local plans in the local library, and sending it to other public bodies such as Oak-leigh Parish Council."

"But that's not public consultation!" I replied, trying to be helpful.

"Look, I'm sorry but I'm not here to discuss cement-mix with you!" At least, that's what I thought she said at the time, although a subsequent session with my dog-eared dictionary at home suggests she might have said that she wasn't there to discuss semantics.

Finally, in response to my question about saving the tree by building around it, I was told that the landscape of-ficer had declared it to be diseased and unfit for preserva-tion. So that sounded like that: euthanasia for trees; King

Henry's Oak was to be for the chop. Now his tree would know how his wives had felt.

The mystery of the 'local plans' going out to so-called public consultation, without anyone in the village being aware of it, perplexed me. Discussions showed that other members of Oakleigh Tree Conservation and Heritage Preservation Group were equally baffled.

After a further telephone call to the Council, I was diverted to the Riverside Public Library at Mudiford. Hidden away in the darkest corner of the least frequented part of the Reference Library was a copy of the elusive plans. There, amid 200 pages of waffle about conserving the local heritage and preserving trees, were town-by-town, village-by-village maps.

The maps themselves were cunningly devised. Unlike an atlas where the top of the page is always north, these maps opted for an informal positioning of north, so that it could be at the top of the page, but equally might be at the bottom, the sides, or the corners of the page, or even haphazardly placed in no particular position. One could be forgiven for believing that the aim seemed to be to disorient any members of the public who accidentally happened to notice this 'public consultation'.

Some of the maps had tiny hatched areas and some were devoid of decoration. And what did the hatching mean? – why, new housing estates.

We were all a bit despondent at the next meeting of Oakleigh Tree Conservation and Heritage Preservation Group, until Jim came up with the idea of contacting the builders direct, and seeing if they could amend their plans. Six eager hands agreed.

The next day, I telephoned Legacy Homes, expecting to get a brush off. Instead they proved quite helpful. I was put through to a Mr Warner, the company's community liaison manager. He explained that the final house-layout had not yet been decided and that as long as they were able to fit seventeen houses of a certain style onto the field, they would be happy to see the tree saved. (What he probably meant was that he couldn't care less about the tree, and that his job as community liaison manager was to get developments through with the minimum of fuss).

I arranged to go and view the plans that evening, and thankfully Jim and Greg were able to join me. Mr Warner proved to be an accomplished persuader, laying out a map showing how it would be impossible to fit in seventeen houses into the irregularly shaped field without removing the oak tree.

Any fewer houses would lose the developers money, or make the new houses too expensive for local people to afford them. He insidiously planted the idea that this latter course of action would inevitably mean young married couples being forced out of the village, commuting yuppies coming in to replace them, and another field somewhere in the village needing to be developed for 'local needs'.

It was very easy to look at the map the 'right' way up, and see the validity of his argument. However, we were gathered around the map, so we looked at it from the sides, and our perspective was slightly different. It struck Jim that an entrance to the houses from Mill Road instead of Kings Ride could completely alter the layout of houses, leaving the oak tree as a central feature of the estate. He put this suggestion to Mr Warner.

"Hmm... interesting," he replied, turning the map through 90 degrees. "Yes, I believe that we could save the tree by using a different access to the site. Of course, the District Council would have to agree to the change of access; all of their discussions have indicated that they favoured Kings Ride."

Three days later, Mr Warner telephoned the good news. The planning officers had agreed with the changes in principle, and even better (for them not us) using the new entrance meant that the developers could build eighteen houses instead of the proposed seventeen.

Puffed up with self importance, and armed with a sketch map, I reported the news to the next committee meeting of the Oakleigh Tree Conservation and Heritage Preservation Group.

"What have you done?" shrieked Mrs Parslip, the Group Treasurer, resident of number 11 Mill Road, and venomous opponent of so much as a dog kennel on the site, let alone any houses.

"Not only have you succeeded in increasing the number of houses when we didn't want any, but the entrance to the estate will now be directly opposite my bedroom window. Every morning when people leave for work they will drive straight at my window, and be able to see me when I am getting out of bed. It's disgusting!"

I had to agree, although it seemed better not to say it at the time. Mrs Parslip is a large woman, indeed a very large woman, with a florid, puffy face, crooked stained teeth, the hair style of a Medusa and demonic eyes. The thought of her getting out of bed as an affliction on anyone leaving the estate was definitely disgusting. Not that I shall be seeing much of Mrs Parslip in the future, as she told us where to stick our tree preservation group.

The rest of the evening remains a blur...of beer, and the quest to persuade one of our dwindling number to become the new treasurer.

CHAPTER TWO

ONE BORN EVERY MINUTE

Some two months had elapsed since we had saved the tree, and the tree vigilantes, sorry, I mean Oakleigh Tree Conservation and Heritage Preservation Group had reverted to a vegetative state under its complacent chairman.

Indeed the events might never have happened or been forgotten in their entirety were it not for a little newspaper cutting from an inside page of our local paper, the Clarion, showing a small group gathered around an ugly misshapen tree under the headline:

VILLAGE ACTIVISTS SAVE
HISTORIC TREE AFTER
COUNCIL COCK-UP.

It was a Sunday morning, around ten thirty. Penny and I sat in our pyjamas, munching on toast and marmalade, while ignoring each other in favour of different sections of the same newspaper. I held the all-important sports section reading a report on the six to nil defeat of Grimchester United, seeking any glimmers of comfort in the performance, if not the score-line, of our local soccer club.

Meanwhile Penny was enthusing over the totally superfluous lifestyle supplement, and a feature on a bathroom so large that we could have fitted the entire furniture contents of our house into it, and still had plenty of room for our ablutions. The actual news section lay on the side, discarded and forgotten.

The sound of the telephone ringing interrupted our thoughts. Silently cursing whoever was ringing up so early on a Sunday morning, I picked up the receiver, as much to cut out the bell sound as to see who was calling.

"Oakleigh 3605," I snarled.

The voice on the other end of the line sounded like a double glazing salesman: "Hello, is it possible to speak to John Edwards of the Oakleigh Tree Conservation and Heritage Preservation Group?"

"Yes, speaking," returned a voice coiled like a cobra, ready to pounce on the first mention of any of those expected keywords like 'special offer' or 'UPVC windows'.

"Good morning. This is Councillor Mike Drinkwater from Stepley. I wonder if I could come over and see you today. It is very important."

"What is?" the voice softening, intrigued now that I was not being offered to have my back windows free if I took advantage of their once-in-a-lifetime deal on front windows and doors.

"Well, it's rather complicated, so I prefer not to go into details on the telephone," the silken voice continued. "Shall we say eleven o'clock?"

"Well, all right," I replied, and the conversation terminated abruptly.

"Who was that dear?" enquired Penny.

"A Councillor Drinkwater. He's coming over to see me in half an hour."

I reached out to pick up the remaining corner of my toast, only to have it snatched out of my hand.

"No time to eat," my animated wife had sprung into action. "You'd better go and put your suit on; you can't meet a councillor in your dressing gown."

"But I don't wear my suit on Sundays," was drowned by the ongoing staccato verbal onslaught.

"It's a pity that they didn't give you more notice, still it can't be helped. I'll just put all of these things in the kitchen. I should just have time to vacuum and clean the bathroom before they arrive."

"But you only did that yesterday" cut no ice.

"Don't forget to comb your hair, it looks a mess. And you'd better shave." The cleaning cyborg, that had been my wife a few moments early, leapt into an overdrive of purposeful action.

Mumbling something about not needing to shave because I had no intention of kissing the councillor, I moved unwillingly in the direction of our non-lifestyle bathroom.

Forty minutes later the doorbell rang, and two of the great and the good introduced themselves before being shepherded into the lounge. Councillor Drinkwater reminded me of Salvador Dali, with black slicked down hair and a stunted Daliesque moustache.

He introduced his companion (accomplice would be a more appropriate word) as Tom Renton, Chairman of the Campaign for Rural Advancement and Protection. This organisation was announced in such a tone that assumed I would surely know what it was. I was too sheepish to say "never heard of it".

"What can I do for you?" was the only obvious question to me. Not so Penny, who had a succession of essential queries: "Tea or coffee?", "Milk?", "Sugar?", "One lump or two?"

In between answering my wife, Dali responded with "Rather, what can we do for you?" He continued: "we were very pleased at your success in saving that tree. We've been making enquiries about you."

"Enquiries about you," piped in Mr Renton, speaking for the first time since confirming the important matters: coffee with milk and two sugars.

"Obviously you have a great love of the countryside, and of your village, of course," Dali elaborated. You're just the kind of person that we've been looking for in Oakleigh. If I may say, we've been looking for a man of your calibre for some time. Am I right or am I right, Tom?"

"You are so very right, Mike," added Tom Renton, who it seemed to me had taken on the appearance of a parrot.

Doubtless a confused look decorated my brow, so Dali continued. "In two months time it's the District Council elections."

"District Council elections," underlined the parrot.

"We're looking for somebody of your stature as our candidate," the councillor continued.

"But I don't know anything about councils or politics. The sum total of my knowledge is a photograph of Margaret Thatcher on my dartboard, and I'm such a bad player that I usually miss that."

"Very droll, very droll," said Dali, feigning amusement. "Nevertheless, you showed great leadership qualities in the matter of the tree, and we already know that you serve on the committee of several local organisations: the school PTA, the youth soccer club, etc."

"Great leadership qualities," reinforced the parrot.

"But John's already got a job – at the bank," Penny leapt to my defence.

"You misunderstand, dear lady," continued Councillor Drinkwater, "the Council only meets about eight times a year, and in the evenings. It won't take up much time at all. It certainly won't interfere in your husband's work, and he would be doing a great service to the local community."

"Great service to the community," piped in the councillor's echo. I expected him to announce "pieces of eight, pieces of eight," at any moment, as I believe his predecessor had done in 'Treasure Island', but he didn't.

Ten minutes later, the deal was done. Always a sucker for flattery, I, John Edwards, was now the official election candidate for an organisation that I'd never even heard of half an hour earlier.

One is tempted at this point to say that great visions swam before the eyes, for despite denial of an interest in politics, like many people, at heart I had always been an armchair politician. Now a new beginning beckoned. To-day Oakleigh. Tomorrow Sleepyvale. And at the weekend, I shall be helping to remould the world as I would like it to be. Well, all of us have our fantasies: bedding Jennifer Aniston or Brad Pitt, scoring the winning goal in the cup final, changing the world.

The next few weeks fairly hurtled by. Hard as I tried, I couldn't think of a single reason why I should run for Council. Unfortunately hard as I racked my brains, I couldn't find a convincing reason not to either. By the time that Mike Drinkwater reappeared clutching a handful of complex official-looking forms, my fate was sealed.

He spread out the all of the papers on our kitchen ta-ble, showing where he had been particularly helpful by putting cross marks in pencil so that I would know where to sign. Nevertheless I insisted on reading each form, just in case he really was a double glazing salesman, and this was a particularly inspired form of deception designed to sign me up as a customer.

He had become a fairly regular visitor in the preced-ing weeks, probably wanting to ensure that I didn't wriggle off of his hook. By the fourth visit, notwithstanding him being a councillor, Penny had decreed that he be allowed in the kitchen, provided that we had an hour's advance 'clearing-up' notice.

Personally I have always tried to sign forms in the kitchen. The light is better, and the backless stools uncom-fortable, so that people on business are less likely to out-stay their welcome.

One of the forms was known as the nomination paper and required that I get the signatures of any ten Oakleigh residents to allow me to stand.

"That shouldn't be difficult," I said confidently. "Penny can sign, Jim and Greg and their wives, the rest of the tree group. Yes ten should be easy enough."

"I'm still not sure that I want you to do this" piped in Penny. "After all you've not been a councillor before; you've got no experience. Supposing you make a bad job of it?"

"Look, love, all councillors start off inexperienced," I replied, unconvinced of the validity of my argument. "Anyway I don't suppose for a moment that I'll win the election."

"Quite right on the first point. But not on the second! You will have the full backing and support of all of the other Campaign for Rural Advancement and Protection Councillors and party activists," added Mike. "Anyway, I'm sure that you'll do a better job than whoever the Tories put up. As for winning, well, we have a secret weapon."

"Are there a lot of your party on our Council then?" asked Penny pertinently.

If it were possible to embarrass a councillor of Mike Drinkwater's standing, then I'm sure that he would have coloured up at this stage. Instead he just cleared his throat.

"Well I'm the only sitting councillor...but we're hopeful of big things at this election." he confided, exuding confidence.

"Returning to this form," he continued. "It would be better if you could get ten different households to sign your nomination papers, rather than get two or three people living in the same house. Ideally, try to get as wide a dispersal as possible, you know, from different parts of the village. It makes the opposition think that you've already got widespread support."

I began to realise that with Penny still voting 'don't know', and Mike's idea to cast a wide net, this form wasn't going to be as easy to complete as I had thought.

"Don't worry," said Mike. "Once you've filled in the forms, I'll go out knocking on doors with you, to get your 'names'. It shouldn't take more than an hour or two."

"What's this form for?" I queried with deep suspicion, looking at a title that read 'Appointment of an Agent'." (Every agent I've ever dealt with: travel agent, literary agent, etc. all seem to want money from me.)

"Oh that's just someone to take care of all of the paperwork for you, as it will all be new to you first time around" Mike reassured.

"And it's not going to cost me anything?"

"No, of course not."

"You're absolutely positive?"

"Absolutely positive. Just fill it in, putting me down as your agent. It then means that I can sort out postal votes, proxy votes, scrutinising representatives and all of the other tedious paperwork."

"By the way," I asked "what's this secret weapon that's going to win us the election? A tank?"

"In a manner of speaking, you could say that he's like a tank; a human tank capable of destroying the opposition. Enough for now, it's my little surprise. Let's just say that I don't think that you'll be disappointed." Councillor Mike Drinkwater positively drooled at the prospect of bringing in his secret weapon.

With the paperwork all duly completed, we set off to persuade ten unsuspecting villagers to sign their names, thereby allowing them the dubious privilege of having a certain *EDWARDS, John Winston, (Campaign for Rural Advancement and Protection)* on the ballot papers for the Oakleigh ward of Sleepyvale District Council.

CHAPTER THREE

ALL'S FAIR IN LOVE AND ELECTIONS

Two days later I was introduced to Councillor Drinkwater's secret weapon – the Campaign for Rural Advancement and Protection's Regional Campaigns Manager.

Arthur Greenleaf was a short stocky individual of indeterminate middle age. He appeared to have no neck, as if his pit-bull-terrier head had been somehow screwed into his torso.

It would be difficult to say whether he actually exhuded power, or whether the deference afforded him by Mike and Tom Renton created the illusion. He was genial enough, but this was overlaid with a gritty determination, which is probably where he acquired his party reputation as 'The Iron Fist in a Velvet Glove'.

"Right John," he started, "I've been brought in to run your election campaign because Oakleigh is our number one target seat in the region. Have you been signed up yet?"

Wondering whether the target seat meant that there was a large bullseye painted on the local farmer's field, I confirmed that I had. "Yes, I've filled in all of the nomination papers, and Mike's acting as my agent."

"No! No! No! Not the Council papers! Have you signed up with the party yet?" A look at my face and the bashful expressions on those of Mike and Tom confirmed that I hadn't.

He pulled out a pad of printed forms. "Pen!" he barked, and Mike and Tom rushed to provide a writing implement, while I was still thinking about where to find one.

"Right, you put your name and address here, then sign and date it. Then you give me a cheque for £14 made payable to the Campaign for Rural Advancement and Protection for this year's membership, and complete this direct debit order from your bank for future annual payments."

The forms were delivered onto the table in a no-nononsense-will-be-allowed manner, like a series of unstoppable blows from a heavyweight boxing champion. I sheepishly signed all of the forms as instructed without my usual safeguard of reading everything first.

"Right"" he said. "Welcome to the party," and he held out his hand supported by a warm welcoming smile. Turning to Mike, he asked, "So who are we up against?"

"There's a new Conservative candidate, and Doris Plummer will be standing for Labour again."

"No Alliance candidate?" queried the campaign 'god'.

"No," replied Mike. "They seem to have made a right cock up of it. The Social Democrats and the Liberals were expected to have agreed a straight split, with each wing of the party fighting half of the seats, the Social Democrats mostly in the towns, and the Liberals in the villages. But neither of them are standing here, while in Westbourne they've got three candidates – one Liberal and Social Democrat, one Social Democrat and one Liberal – anti Alliance."

"Good, that gives us a clear run at gathering in all of the protest votes here," summarised a pleased Arthur. "John, how do you feel about your opponents?"

"I don't really know them," I replied unhelpfully.

"No! No! No! Not on a personal basis! How do you feel about their politics?"

I thought for a moment before giving what I hoped would be a sagacious reply. "They're well meaning individuals with slightly different views to my own," I ventured.

"No! No! No!!" Arthur stamped his fist on the table to emphasis his disapproval. "They are the enemy! Do you want to be a nice guy, or a winner?"

"Can't I be both?" I asked somewhat naively.

"Impossible," replied Arthur. "Your job is to convince as many people as possible in the village that you're the right man to be their councillor. It's no good being 'Mr Wishy Washy Nice Guy'. You need to be utterly ruthless. You must do everything in your power to destroy your opponents' political credibility. That way you become their sole hope."

"But surely that damages my own credibility?" I queried.

"No! No! No! Not at all!" reassured Arthur, "Right, Mike, what was the result last time?"

Councillor Drinkwater opened a thick file and thumbed through to the result which he read aloud in a booming voice, as if declaring it for the first time:

"Conservatives 282, Liberals 61, Feline Protection League 28, Labour 16."

'God' slowly repeated the result as he wrote it down on a little notepad, adding a few subtle changes:

"Tories 282, Liberals 61, Others 28, Labour 16."

"Is that what we are? 'Other'?" I asked in an attempt to lighten the oppressive atmosphere.

Athur responded with the reactions of a striking cobra.

"We are not Other! We are the Campaign for Rural Advancement and Protection, the only national party that will do anything to help your village. Remember that, and spread the word."

Perhaps more than anything else he had said, this last phrase with its Messiahic timbre reinforced the view of the others in the room that here was no mere mortal, but at the very least a prophet, if not a god among men.

Later that evening I wrote my 'election address', which had nothing to do with where I lived, where the Council offices were, or where one voted. It was designed to be a friendly open letter to my fellow villagers pledging to work for the good of the village, and was to go on one side of my election leaflet.

I gave my copy to Mike the following day. He looked somewhat perplexed by its political naiveté, although he admitted that it looked as though it was written 'from the heart'. He showed me the other side of the leaflet which was a savage attack on the present Tory administration for spending all of the Council's money on towns like Mudiford, and its failure to protect the rural areas from development.

It went on to raise the spectre of a Labour party that in Grimchester had 'wasted' a fortune on gays, blacks, new age travellers, Trade Union militants, jaunts by councillors to 'Communist' Eastern Europe and the Caribbean, and suchlike 'threats to decent society and our way of life'.

Finally, the Alliance were mauled as a disorganised hotch-potch in which every candidate came from a different party and had a different view on everything. These last comments seemed particularly irrelevant as they weren't even putting up a candidate, but Mike explained to me that this side of the leaflet would be used throughout the district and that it was only the election address side that changed from village to village. The whole leaflet was littered with blood-curdling pictures to support the text. Finally, at the foot of the page was a tiny section about the Campaign for Rural Advancement and Protection policies. As if anybody was going to read that far down.

I queried the whole tone of the page. "Shouldn't we be a bit more constructive in promoting our own policies, rather than criticising others?"

Mike looked a little confused by the question.

"Whatever for? Most people aren't particularly interested in our individual policies. They like to hear what's wrong with the others, and to be reassured that at least we will be looking after their best interests. That way they'll vote for us."

I must admit that the councillor's logic was far above my head, and I was relieved that at least my side of the leaflet was written constructively.

A few days later, Arthur 'God' Greenleaf and I prepared to deliver our leaflets, an act familiar to me through the delivery of our leaflets to start up Oakleigh Tree Conservation and Heritage Preservation Group, now seemingly aeons away.

"Now John," Arthur stated. "It's most important that you post your leaflets all the way through the letterboxes."

"Yes understood," I replied. "Presumably so that burglars won't know that there's nobody in."

This puzzled Arthur somewhat, so he enlightened me. "No! No! No! It's to stop the other parties from taking your leaflets out of the letterboxes."

"Surely they don't do things like that?" I asked in the naive belief that there must be some kind of code of decency among councillors, as there was 'honour among thieves'.

"Of course they do! I do! Everyone does!" Obviously the party's Supreme Being wasn't all sweetness and light as the party faithful seemed to think, and thought nothing of cheating to achieve his ends.

"Well I'm not going to!" I responded in my most indignant voice, seizing the initiative over my illustrious tutor. "The people have a right to hear what the other candidates say. Anyway it's their mail. We shouldn't steal it."

"You're going to make it very difficult to win this seat from the Tories if you're going to be honest and upright all of the time!" thundered Arthur, spitting out the word 'Tories' as if he had something unpleasant in his mouth.

We set off on our first walk together, posting leaflets at alternate houses. We had obviously followed a fairly inept Labour leafleteer who had left large numbers of their leaflets stuck halfway out of the letterboxes. I added mine and pushed both all of the way through. I couldn't say whether this was a simple act of defiance at sharp practice, or whether it was to stop any later Conservative leafleteer from removing both of their rivals' literature in one fell swoop.

It would have been pleasant to record that Arthur's conscience had been likewise pricked, but presumably he had no such qualms. He seemed to be suspiciously foraging in letterboxes like a squirrel hunting for its winter nuts, and by the end of the evening his pockets were bulging in a manner in which they had not at the beginning.

With only the two of us, and a commitment to deliver to every house, flat and farm, it took us three successive evenings to deliver all of our leaflets, more exercise than I had enjoyed since my schooldays. (I use the word enjoyed reservedly for an activity that left me hot and sweaty, with sore feet and an aching back.)

However, it was educational. It reinforced my memory of a couple of months earlier of just how many inconsiderate people choose to put their letterboxes just two inches above their doormats, and how many keep snarling dogs ready to pounce on any politician's fingers if they pushed their leaflets all of the way through the letterbox. Maybe the Labour leafletter had more experience than I gave him credit for.

Arthur would stop from time to time, flashing his large green and white rosette as he admired people's gardens, however meticulous or tawdry they appeared. He would introduce me as "well-known local campaigner John Edwards who had single-handedly saved King Henry's Oak from the Tory axe."

I would then shake hands and shyly flash my little rosette. This was the same colour as Arthur's but only half the size. However, it did have the word 'candidate' on it in large black letters. I couldn't help but mentally compare this with those slips of paper marked 'kick me' that we would attach to the back of other kids' jackets at school. This reaction was heightened at those houses whose response to being offered a leaflet was to tell us things such as, "Drop it in the dustbin, on the way out, with the rest of them."

Obviously there were a reasonable number of my fellow villagers unwilling even to read my carefully composed election address, and who firmly believed that the right and proper place for my leaflets, as well as that of Labour and the Conservatives, was as mere fodder for a landfill site.

CHAPTER FOUR

UNDER CANVAS –
THE ELECTION CAMPAIGN CONTINUES

On the day following the final leaflet drop, I was press-ganged into something called canvassing, which had nothing whatsoever to do with tents.

Arthur was insistent about the need to knock on every door in the village, shake every hand and find out the voting intention of every owner.

There would only be the two of us, since Tom was carrying out a similar process in helping Mike to retain his 'safe' seat. One might wonder why they bothered if it was a 'safe' seat. Apparently even constituents who had no intention of voting, expected their April evening spent slaving over a hot TV to be interrupted by the dreaded knock on the door of one or more members of the brigade of genial rosette wearers.

I had hoped to get some assistance from the much vaunted party 'helpers', but they seemed to be permanently unavailable to help.

Mike had supplied us with a complete list of every villager with columns alongside their names to tick off their voting intentions.

It would be extremely boring to the reader, at this juncture, to give a blow-by-blow, doorbell-by-doorbell account of every response. Suffice it to say that about half of the time it was a question of embellishing a particular party's box, and the rest of the time ticking the ProbC., DK and NV boxes. Unless I had a particular reason for thinking otherwise (such as a Labour poster in the window), I was instructed by Arthur to tick ProbC whenever the person answering the door declined to own up to their political loyalties, but it was obvious that they had already decided.

ProbC stood for probable Conservatives. Arthur explained that their coyness was because they were ashamed to admit that they were Maggie's lot, or Maggots as he graphically described Conservative supporters. I kept quiet, although I did wonder whether they were just telling us to 'mind your own business' in the politest way that they knew.

DK stood for Don't Know and NV for Not Voting. The way that Arthur described it, the difference was minimal. NVs would not vote, while DKs would not vote either, they simply didn't know it yet. Had a DN-NV coalition been standing, they would have swept into power, because they enjoyed such widespread support.

NV supporters championed their cause in a variety of ways. There was the curt "We don't vote," through an increasingly hostile range of opinions culminating in: "Yer all useless bastards tarred with the same brush." For someone who had entered this gladiatorial contest for no other reason than to benefit the village, this hostile apathy was somewhat disconcerting.

Of course, not all of the responses were so unfriendly. At one house, a pleasant enough lady explained that "We're Jehovah's Witnesses, so we don't vote."

When I joked that "It made a change, me knocking on your door," she seemed completely baffled about what I meant.

I declined the opportunity to try to persuade them to join the Holy Church of the Voters, or to sell them a copy of 'Watchvillage' or whatever our party's information/ recruitment leaflet might be called. Instead I mused whether they knew what the Council did on their behalf. Did they think that, now God had plenty of time on his hands after finishing his six-day shift of world creation, He popped around and emptied their dustbins every Thursday before moving onto other duties.

DN supporters may be generally summarised as polite ditherers. Comments such as, "I haven't really thought about it."; "I didn't know that there was an election,"; and "I'll have to ask my husband" seemed to indicate that this was indeed the moderate wing of the NV.

However, in the midst of this extravaganza of apathy there were a few interesting 'meetings', of which I will recount just three.

Arthur had told me to be short and sweet, and keep moving. Otherwise he feared we might not finish the canvass. Unfortunately for his ambitions, if people wanted to discuss things with me I was happy to do so, and pleased that they were taking an interest.

On the first evening, one of the houses where I knocked was opened by a desperately thin-looking man with a wispy beard and a hunted expression in his eyes.

After I had introduced myself, he ventured a question of his own. "So what do you think about nuclear weapons?"

I was somewhat caught off-guard by a question so remote from the kind of local issues that I might be able to influence on the Council.

"Well, it's not really relevant to the District Council" I ventured. After pausing for thought, I added a personal opinion. "I suppose nuclear weapons are a necessary evil. At least they've succeeded in stopping a major war in Europe for nearly fifty years."

This goaded the questioner to a response. "So you think that it is all right that we have weapons of mass destruction, capable of wiping out all life on the planet?"

I tried to be statesman-like in dealing with this attack. "Well hopefully the very real threat posed by that destruction is our best guarantee of it never happening, and our best guarantee of peace in the future."

My elector was suitably unimpressed. "You talk about peace, yet you favour retaining overwhelming military might. You're nothing but a warmonger. It's people like you that started the last two world wars!"

It was at this point that Arthur's wisdom leapt to my salvation, and I made a polite as swift as exit as I could.

A few evenings later, occurred the most unusual interview of the canvass. Arthur had continually drummed into me the need to identify the person at the door to ensure that they were on the electoral roll. I hadn't really got into the swing of it. For example, if the person answering the door was a decrepit old man with a tobacco stained moustache, and he readily indicated his support for one or other of my boxes, I simply ticked accordingly alongside *WEATHERSPOON, Earnest Mafeking Kitchener*, and assumed that was who I had been speaking to.

At one neatly painted house with a precise if fussy garden, the door was opened by a beautiful tall redhead. She was dressed in a bright red, full-length silk kimono with golden decorations and long splits in the skirt from which a shapely knee and long leg provocatively protruded. Her face was lovely in a slightly unusual way that I couldn't really describe, and her subtle make-up was immaculate under the gorgeous scarlet ringlets that cascaded down her back.

Are you sure that it's only my VOTE that you're after.

"Erm... I'm John Edwards... your Campaign for Rural Advancement and Preservation candidate in the District Elections... I... I wonder if I can count on your support?" I muttered, having suddenly developed a stammer.

"Well John," she breathed in a husky voice that exhuded a sexuality enhanced by the rising of her bosom through the thin silk material, "perhaps you'd like to come in and discuss it over coffee?"

Wondering how my more illustrious colleagues would have responded, I accepted shyly, then looked around furtively to make sure that I wasn't being watched, before stepping inside. I was initially relieved when we sat down for coffee that the lovely creature sat opposite me rather than next to me on the sofa. That was until she began crossing her legs this way and that; each time the slit in her skirt going higher and higher.

"So John," she whispered huskily, "if I agree to give you what you want, can I guarantee that you will completely satisfy me."

"Pardon?" I mumbled.

"If I give it to you – my vote, will I be satisfied?"

Relieved that the conversation had almost moved on from innuendo, I assured the vision of loveliness that I would do my best.

"So you will always try to give me what I want? If I need you, you will come day or night?" she breathed, emphasising the word 'come'.

I struggled to find the right response. "Well, I will make myself available as much as possible."

"So you would do your best to service me?" she laughed, lifting one dainty foot onto the couch and hugging her bare knee, with the result that the split in her skirt slid almost to her crotch.

In response, I blushed.

"Well John," she said at last, "I've decided that you can have me."

As she declared her intent, she ran the thumb and middle finger of her left hand slowly up and down her coffee cup in a very suggestive manner.

"Yes," she continued, "I couldn't possibly vote Labour; their candidate looks like an extra in the Rovers Return. I have to admit that I was tempted by the Conservative candidate. He has silver grey hair. I like men with silver grey hair. It's so distinguished. And, naturally, being a Conservative, he's probably utterly depraved behind his chintz curtains. Hmm, how delicious. I like men who are utterly depraved. But then I said to myself, no, Davidia

Charlotte Cornwall, this is the one. He may not have the experience of the Conservative, but he's a nice Big Boy. He's keen and he's got balls. He's unashamedly looked up your skirt all of the time he was talking to you, but he's politely kept his hands in his lap so that you can't be shocked by his reaction. So that's it, John. You can have me. And if you want me to help you out with your erection..."

Here she stopped for a moment before continuing. "I'm sorry, if you need any help with your election, I'm very willing. You needn't ring the bell, just walk down the side of the house and knock on the back door. It's a personal whim. It pleases me that all of my best friends favour back door entry."

Being tongue-tied while at the same time thanking her profusely, I beat a hasty retreat, full of questions and self doubts. How would I respond if she called upon my 'services'. Could a councillor be struck-off for a dalliance with a constituent? After all, doctors can for a fling with a patient. Even more worrying, how would Penny respond if she knew that I was visiting this delightful, ticking, sex bomb?"

I almost forgot to tick any of the boxes on my form, only just remembering as I closed her gate. Looking at the address, I prepared to put an 'ours' cross alongside the only voter listed there, and was visibly shaken by the name: CORNWALL, David Charles.

There were just a few days to go to the election as Arthur and I prepared for our last bout of canvassing – at the outlying farms.

"Well," I said, "I am pleased now that this is almost over. We've been out virtually every night and all weekends for the past month. I'm beginning to forget what Penny and the kids look like."

"Well yes," retorted Arthur, whose idea of a good

night out was putting leaflets through letterboxes, or knocking on other people's doors, "But it's hardly over yet."

"But we've only got the farms to do and we're finished," I argued hopefully.

"No! No! No! Once the farms are done, we start the second canvass, going back to all of the houses whose occupiers were out the first time. Yes, during the next few days we must redouble our efforts – start earlier, walk faster, finish later."

Someone in the room groaned, and it certainly wasn't that enthusiastic maestro of elections Arthur Greenleaf.

The first farm we visited was the smallholding known as Kings Ridge Farm. After going through my opening spiel, the farmer smiled genially before responding.

"Ah yes. You're the man who's tried to save the tree. Well," he continued, "I don't usually vote – I've got far more important things to do, but as you are at least trying to do something, I suppose this is a special case. I think I'll vote for you."

"Thank you," I replied earnestly. "But why do you say that I've tried to save the tree? We've saved it."

"That you've not," replied the smallholder. "You've only postponed the tree's demise. If you knew more about the rural countryside you want to protect then you would have seen the tree is rotten right through with that Dutch Elm Disease."

"Dutch Elm Disease?" I replied with amazement. "I didn't know that could affect oak trees."

"I don't think it can," confirmed the farmer. "I'm sure you're right there. It doesn't affect oak trees. But then of course, it's an elm tree that you've been trying to save."

"An elm tree?" I queried with astonishment. "But surely it's King Henry's Oak."

"It is."

51

"But you just said that it was an elm tree."

"Yes, it certainly is an elm tree."

I tried to wade through my confusion. "How can it be both? A cross-breed tree?"

"No, of course not. It's always been an elm tree and I have been farming hereabouts nigh on..." he paused for a digression into mental arithmetic "...nigh on 42 years. I don't know much about local history, so I don't know whether King Henry ever came here, or whether an oak tree grew afterwards. What I can say is that tree has never seen an acorn in its life, and what is more, it's never going to.

"If people want to tell the story about King Henry's Oak to get American tourists to come here, that's no business of mine. But I tell you straight. It is an elm tree. It always has been an elm tree. And it always will be an elm tree. But not for much longer. Dutch Elm Disease is like a cancer eating it away."

What little appetite I had left for the remaining canvass had somehow drained away with the ghastly news that my first act for the local community had somehow only postponed the demise of King Henry's 'Elm' tree.

CHAPTER FIVE

E. DAY

At 10 p.m. on the eve of the election, Arthur sat down in the kitchen to discuss the next day's actions and the likely result. On paper the prospects of the Campaign for Rural Advancement and Preservation looked ready to win the seat from the Conservatives by a landslide.

A compilation of all of our canvas sheets produced the following result:

Ours 279

Conservatives 141

Probable Conservatives 57

Labour 9

Liberals/SDP/Alliance 4, even though they weren't standing.

Not Voting/Don't Know 405

"Hmm," mused Arthur, "That puts us neck-and-neck with the Tories."

Bemused, I asked why since even with all of the ProbCs. voting for them, the Conservatives looked a long way behind us.

"Ah" replied Arthur "that's because of the built-in inaccuracy factor. Let's see the likely result using the Liebermann calculation. Firstly we take off a third of the people who said that they would vote for you. That brings us down to 186."

"Why won't they vote for us if they said that they would? A sudden change of heart?" I queried.

"No! No! No! They never were going to vote for you."

"Then why did they say that they would?" I persisted.

"To get us off of their doorstep I imagine" came back Arthur's pithy reply, before continuing: "Now add on two thirds of the ProbCs. to the Tories makes them 179. Yes it's certainly going to be very close: 186 to 179."

My huge majority seemed to have disappeared somewhere thanks to the calculations of Messrs. Greenleaf and Liebermann.

"Never mind," said Arthur reassuringly. "As long as we get our vote out on the day we can still win."

"Get our vote out?" I queried.

"Yes, you know, going around and knocking on people's doors to tell them to vote. It's one of those European soccer matches live on television tomorrow, so it's bound to be a lower turnout than usual. Of course most of the women will still vote, if only to get away from the football. And they'll be mostly Tory. Sort of handbag solidarity movement with Maggie."

"What, knock on every one's door?" I asked with incredulity.

"No! No! No! Only those who said that they would vote for you."

"But how can we tell if they're really going to vote for me, or if they just wanted to get rid of me?" I asked with a sense of foreboding about what the next day was likely to be like.

"You can't. But if we knock them all up, then two thirds of them are likely to vote for us." Arthur seemed positively cheerful at the prospect.

I had been persuaded against my better judgement of the need to take election day off as a holiday from my job at the bank. Suddenly the alternative attractions of arranging direct debits, carrying out security checks and counting out notes and weighing coins for the usual Thursday wage cheques being cashed, seemed a really attractive alternative.

"Right!" continued Arthur enthusiastically. "I've arranged for you to pick up our 'Good Morning' leaflets from the Mudiford Printing Company at five-thirty tomorrow morning. I'm sure that you won't mind, but you'll need to pay them £86 for the printing. As you've not yet contributed to the election costs it's by way of your contribution to the election fighting fund so to speak. All in a good cause. All in a good cause.

Now I'll be around by six o'clock, so that we can fold the leaflets. We're not really supposed to deliver before seven, so we need to be up and ready to start dead on time."

The news that I'd be paying for yet another leaflet was a pretty unwelcome body-blow to my rapidly diminishing enthusiasm. Somehow paying for new double glazing didn't seem such a bad idea after all.

"It's a pity," 'God' mused, "that we didn't realise that it was going to be this close beforehand."

"Why, what difference would that make?" I queried.

"Well, we might have been able to dig up some dirt on your opponent. I remember fighting Whittlesea last year. We'd got a good local candidate, but he looked like being badly beaten into second place by the sitting councillor. Then I had the foresight to empty the councillor's dustbin a couple of weeks before the election. That provided me with a really juicy story for the local press. Then – Wham! Bang! We were in by a landslide."

"I don't really think that I would want to win that way" I answered indignantly. "Anyway I have no intention of rummaging through other people's dustbins."

"Tch, tch, tch. Tetchy. I've told you before" said Arthur. "Do you want to be a nice guy or a winner? Nice guys get forgotten. Winners rewrite history."

Somehow the idea of playing even a minor role in history had become very unappetising.

The next day it rained hard. But then it would, wouldn't it?

I crept out of the house just after 5 a.m. and drove the ten miles to the printers, who were unreasonably cheerful at such an ungodly hour. Grudgingly I handed over a cheque in exchange for a large box on the outside of which a copy of the contents had been taped. The words 'Good Morning' were emblazoned in black on a vivid green fluorescent paper. As the parcel sat in the passenger seat it seemed to be mocking me as I drove back home through the driving rain.

I returned home for a black coffee, the second of many that were to follow that day. I had barely finished making it when there was a thunderous knocking on the front door, guaranteed to wake up the family, if not the dead. Arthur had obviously been drinking from the same nectar as the printers. He was buoyed up with enthusiasm at the coming conflict and chatted away gleefully as we folded leaflets.

Upstairs there had been some discernible movement, but obviously a quick look at the clock was sufficient for them to drift back to sleep.

An hour later we began our deliveries.

The wind howled. The rain drove into our faces, stinging us with its ferocity. I wondered if some higher power was trying to give us a message. If so, it wasn't lost on me, but it was on Arthur who seemed oblivious to the conditions as he chugged around like an enthusiastic bloodhound in search of fugitive votes. I envied the grumpy milkman with his white cap, and the paper boys and girls on their bicycles. At least they hadn't had to pay for the milk and the newspapers that they were delivering.

As the morning wore on, a few more villagers began to brave the elements. First came the commuters scurrying through the rain to their cars for the short drive to the railway stations at Grimchester or Mudiford. Then the day-shift at Portuguesa Sardines turned out to catch the company-bus link. Next came doting mothers with their offspring shepherding them into all-protecting cars or huddled with them under giant umbrellas, for the short trip to school. Finally came the procession of the senior citizens: those worthies who delighted in telling how, in the 'good old days', they walked twenty miles barefoot through the snow to start at work at six in the morning. They were certainly not in a rush these mornings, barefoot or shod.

Meanwhile Arthur kept up his unrelenting pace thick and fast, posting soggy green paper through letterboxes with the excitement of a child on Christmas Eve.

The seconds stretched to minutes.

The minutes stretched to hours.

The hours seemed to stretch to eternity.

Abruptly, at 11.30, dynamo Greenleaf stopped.

"Right," he said, "Time to stop."

Relieved, I looked around for the nearest dustbin to dispose of my remaining leaflets.

"What are you doing?" he queried, alarmed.

"Throwing away the rest of the leaflets?" I ventured, hopefully stating the obvious.

"No! No! No!" replied Arthur. "This is just a short break. You're telling at the village hall from twelve to two."

"Telling? Telling what? Telling who?" came back the response, not having a clue what he was talking about.

"Telling! Collecting electoral roll numbers," Arthur enlightened.

Unbeknown to me, whilst we had been on our expedition to find the lost tribe of Oakleigh letterboxes, some other unfortunate had been sitting in the rain at the village hall.

Arthur hurried me home for a quick change into 'something smarter', although 'something drier' was my chief priority.

Half a cup of scalding black coffee and a quick call of nature were interrupted by cast-iron-bladder Arthur calling out: "Don't be long. We don't want to be late."

Convicts destined for transportation probably had as much enthusiasm for their move as I had for mine from a warm, cosy kitchen. Nevertheless in next to no time we were outside the village hall where a sodden poster reminded passing villagers that for one day, and one day only, it was their polling station.

A poor old lady who looked about eighty, whom I had never met, handed me her telling sheets, her fingers immobile due to the cold. Somehow I remembered to thank her for her assistance, before taking over her seat. Arthur hurried her away in his car, while I sat in the rain pretending to be keen while collecting the numbers of the few voters who trickled in. If time during leafleting had seemed slow, waiting for the odd visitor to the village hall seemed to have stopped it completely.

I introduced myself to the lady sitting next to me who sported a smart blue rosette.

"Of course," she said in a conciliatory manner, as if she felt sorry for me fighting a lost cause, "we always win Oakleigh. Always have. Always will."

There's nothing that perks up a true Englishman like staring in the face of defeat. We lost many of our most memorable battles, such as Hastings and Dunkirk, and the least said about our sporting prowess the better. Let's just say that we invariably remember when we nearly won any, and how we were cheated out of victory. As a Grimchester United fan, something I am well used to. So, far from being downcast, this perked me up a bit, as if the Dunkirk spirit had somehow popped up out of a puddle. "Well, I'm going to give you a run for your money."

She smiled in a condescending 'poor dear' manner. Soon afterwards she was relieved by a bullish man with a ruddy complexion who smelt strongly of whisky.

He staggered and almost fell down when he was relieved an hour later by a very thin lady wearing one of those folding plastic macs with matching hood. She was carrying a small white poodle that snarled every time it saw the colour of my rosette. Come to think of it, her dog growled at all of our customers as they wandered past clutching their polling cards, so perhaps it was nothing to do with the rosette after all.

In between these changes of personnel, there had been a string of blue rosette wearers arriving to remove their collected numbers. Mine remained unwanted.

I ventured to strike up a conversation with the thin lady by mentioning that I hadn't seen their candidate yet.

"Goodness me, no, nor will you," she confided. "Graeme's far too busy to waste his time fighting the election. I don't think that he's even been to Oakleigh since the election campaign started."

I stated what seemed the obvious, but couldn't resist adding a rider. "Well, I hope that he'll take a keener interest IF he's elected."

"Oh yes," she confirmed, "He's always done very well for us in the past when he's stood."

"Oh, I didn't know that he'd represented Oakleigh before. As he wasn't your sitting councillor, I thought perhaps he was a new candidate."

"Oh no," she replied, "He's never represented Oakleigh before, but he has represented several other places.

At the moment, he's a councillor for one of the Mudiford wards, but they've built an estate of that awful social housing there. The place is full of blacks, gypsies and Communists, so Graeme's swapped wards. Oakleigh is a far safer bet for him."

"So what did you mean when you said he'd done well in the past? Well for his constituents?" I persisted, despite the threat from the poodle curling its lip in a menacing manner.

"Why...? Well, for the party, of course." The good lady's honesty was to be commended, if not the sentiment.

I ascended my high horse: "But what about the village? What will he do for Oakleigh?"

This last question seemed a little too difficult for her to answer so, like a true politician, she changed the question.

"Graeme will make sure that the taxpayers' money is spent wisely."

Our verbal combat could best be likened to trying to get a winkle out of its shell with a blunt matchstick. "Well we will at least see him in the village on a regular basis IF he wins," I tried to confirm.

"Oh no," she replied. "Graeme wouldn't like that. He said that people will only come and pester him with their problems. That's why he's careful never to represent the village in which he lives. It would be too easy for the wrong sort of local people to get hold of him. He'd find that very annoying."

The Dogs of War clashed at the polling station.

The poodle seemed to sense the mood of the interrogation more than his mistress, and as he bared his teeth he fixed me with an eye that was pure venom.

"But I thought that was what councillors were for?" I continued naively.

"Oh no. Graeme says that what the electorate like best is to choose somebody that will make all of the decisions on their behalf, and then not bother them again for four years. Like he does."

I would have continued to probe further, but at that moment Arthur arrived back with his little lady. Casting daggers from his eyes at me for talking to the enemy, I expected him to launch into a fierce barking match with the poodle at any moment.

"Right," said Arthur. "We'll drop these telling sheets to your house, and then carry on with the leaflet drop."

"But the leaflets say 'Good Morning,'" I threw in, desperately searching for an escape route.

"Just another hour," replied Arthur. "Then we'll start knocking up."

"No chance of an afternoon nap then." I answered my own question with a grim face.

When I returned to my house, I was greeted with large green stickers on the windows proclaiming it to be a 'Committee Room'. Inside our lounge-cum-dining room had been transformed.

The dining table had rows of sheets in triplicate containing the list of every voter in Oakleigh who had pledged support.

Arthur introduced me to Sally Greenleaf, his wife and chief architect of the paper piles. She was a lively slim lady dressed in bright green slacks and a bold green and white striped sweatshirt. Probably in her early thirties, Sally would have been ordinary looking but her face, beaming with enthusiasm and satisfaction at her handiwork, made her moderately attractive. I certainly wondered why Arthur didn't want to spend more of his evenings curled up with her on the sofa, rather than interrupting unsuspecting apathetics as they dozed fitfully in front of their favourite television programmes.

Sally took our lists, and began eagerly crossing off names.

I found a harassed Penny in the kitchen having been relegated to sandwiches-and-tea-making for the helpers who were drifting in for their knocking up lists.

"I'm getting a bit fed up with all this," she announced somewhat crossly.

"Me too," I confirmed. "At least it's only for one day,"

I continued, crossing my fingers behind my back.

Seeing Arthur wander into the kitchen, Penny reverted to the ever-polite hostess. "What would you like for lunch?"

"Nothing my dear, thank you. We've no time to eat. Come along John."

Arthur purposefully left the kitchen, and I followed behind like Mary's little lamb.

The nightmare continued for the rest of the day.

Leafleting was followed by three runs for the elderly and infirm unable to make the village hall under their own steam. Then came ringing on bells and knocking on doors to intimidate very reluctant villagers into carrying out their civic duty at the ballot box. For those foolish residents who had said, when canvassed, that they would support every candidate, they faced the spectre of one different coloured rosette after another coming down their path. They must have wondered why they were being persecuted so much.

Still only a few more hours, and the polls would close. I was really looking forward to getting my feet up in front of a roaring fire.

CHAPTER SIX

OUT FOR THE COUNT

Arthur kept up his relentless election day pace. Even when there were only a few minutes to close of poll, he could still be found ringing doorbells with unbounded enthusiasm.

Sally performed with equal fanaticism. Like a workaholic counter assistant at the Post Office, she took telling sheets, crossed off names from her list and sent out her half-a-dozen helpers with relish and knocking up lists. (Not, of course, that there is such a beast as a workaholic Post Office-counter assistant. They are as mythical as unicorns, elves and benign businesspersons.)

By no stretch of the imagination could my attempts at knocking up be described as anything less than disastrous. Although I set off enthusiastically, this was quickly dampened, and not by the rain.

Virtually everyone on my list was either out, claimed to have already voted, or decided that they weren't going to vote after all. In the midst of all this activity I was still getting comments such as: "I didn't realise there was an election on" and "Are you sure it's today, I thought it was next month?"

Returning home, the hoped for cup of coffee was not forthcoming. Instead Sally greeted me with a welcome smile that an air hostess would have been proud of, before giving me a few more pages listing the names of those who hadn't yet voted.

I managed to get a bit of a rest from this frenetic activity, as Arthur had put me back on telling at the village hall from six o'clock to eight. He thought it was a good idea to have the candidate showing himself as keen. This theme was continued afterwards as I was trotted out to harass the tardiest of our potential supporters, although I suspect that this was as effective as opening up with the big guns at the Battle of the Somme.

I sat next to an affable man of pensionable age, who turned out to be a parish councillor. Despite his adornment of a large blue rosette, he told me at least three times that he wasn't a Conservative (or any other political party supporter for that matter). He insisted that he was only 'helping out' and I thought it somewhat churlish to pursue the matter.

My spell at the polling station coincided with the busiest time of the day. Arthur called it 'the rush', although this didn't seem a particularly appropriate accolade since nobody seemed to be rushing in to vote with enthusiastic zeal. 'The amble' would have been a more appropriate title, since most people seemed to amble in with faces betraying their disinterest. I've seen a queue in a dentists' waiting room with as much enthusiasm as the electorate of Oakleigh. The only rushing was when they came out, as they scurried away as if to say 'thank goodness that's over for another year'.

Faces came and went including quite a few that I recognised. This cheered me up a bit despite the rain. At least it made me think that all of the work had been worthwhile after all.

Jim and Greg both went in, relieving me of the difficult task of getting them out of the Pig and Crown once my shift had finished. Likewise other members of the Oakleigh Tree Conservation and Heritage Group came and went. Greg pretended that he didn't recognise me. Perhaps he thought that you weren't supposed to know the candidates on a personal basis, or maybe he was a life-long supporter of one of the main parties standing against me.

The sagacious farmer went through with a friendly "You've got my vote."

One other face that looked vaguely familiar belonged to a tall man, immaculately dressed in a pinstripe suit.

"Could I have your number please?" I asked politely.

"Oh! Fancy you not recognising one of your most ardent supporters, you naughty big boy," he replied laughing. "Don't you remember me? David Cornwall."

The polling station closed, and the staff brought out their day's work in a black-metal padlocked box. It was put into a waiting car from where it made the short drive to Mudiford Leisure Centre and the count which was to take place in the main gymnasium.

I was feeling pretty ragged and would have liked a shower and change of clothes before joining the count. Unfortunately Arthur insisted that we went as we were because we didn't have enough time.

He and Sally both looked radiant, as if they had enjoyed some deliciously erotic experience, rather than a day's electioneering. Penny had somehow managed to bunk off from sandwich-making half an hour earlier, and looked resplendent in a smart new dress. At least I think it was new as I didn't recognise it although, to confess, the full contents of her wardrobe remain as much a mystery to me as the workings of her female brain.

So it was to be no more than a quick cup of tepid tea and a 'Ham Sandwich á la British Rail'. Despite Penny's best endeavours, the heat of the election in our house had curled up the corners in the style that this renowned culinary provider would have approved of. Then the four of us were off for the final act of the day.

The main gymnasium of Mudiford Leisure Centre had been transformed. The sign warning sports persons about only wearing shoes with soft soles, excluding those with black soles, remained. However, it had been totally ignored.

Instead there was a sea of smartly dressed individuals, who were mostly candidates and other members of the political hierarchy, backed by a substantial number wearing jeans, anoraks and suchlike working clobber, who I was told were activists. I later understood this to mean the party faithful who did all of the work, whilst their supposed betters were slaving over wine and cheese parties.

Almost all manner of footwear was on display, from stiletto heels to working boots, many seemingly especially designed to inflict the maximum possible damage on the delicate wooden floor. Only one kind of footwear appeared noticeably absent. There didn't seem to be a trainer in sight, with black or any other colour sole.

The badminton nets, gymnasium mats, trampolines, and other paraphernalia had all been spirited away. In their place were rows of trestle tables, three tables in each row, covered with garishly coloured plastic covers, their black metal legs all grinding away at the floorboards. At the end of each row of tables a sheet of paper had been taped showing the village or area of the town being counted there. The rows had been arranged in a kind of irregular rectangle-cum-semi-circle. It reminded me of a giant wagon train stockade. On the inside of the tables sat the 'cowboys': rows of bored looking council staff, their friends and family, and anyone else they could drag in to help with the count. Outside of the stockade there were groups of fierce looking 'Indians', all of them savages fanatically devoted to their own tribe. Their chests were adorned with a unique kind of warpaint made of cardboard and ribbons, and each tribe had its own tribal colour or combination of colours.

The Bluefoot and Redskin tribes predominated. They were almost matched numerically by a coalition of minor tribes who had grouped together for strength. Half of these sported a positive vignette of every shade imaginable in yellow, gold and orange. The other half were a group of renegade Redskins, now decked out in red, white and blue to stake their independence.

Apart from the main warrior bands, there were a few smaller tribes to break up the monotony of colour. Taking great care to avoid a small gathering painted uniquely in green, Arthur steered us carefully through the other warbands to a clump of our allies sporting warpaint in green and black, and green and white.

"How! Me Grey Wolf!" I showed the palm of my hand as I introduced myself good humouredly to a member of my tribe that I didn't recognise.

"How! Me Agent for Mudiford Riverside Ward!" he replied. He began to raise his own hand in the traditional Red Indian salutation, realised what he was doing, put it down abruptly and gave me a perplexed look while tut-tutting at his own gullibility.

After we had exchanged real names, positions and wards, Arthur shepherded the four of us to the table marked 'Oakleigh'. We took up our positions on the attacking side of the wagons from where we could see the whites of the eyes of those palefaces designated to count the voting slips.

The Deputy Returning Officer was surrounded by warring tribes in blue, red, yellow and green warpaint.

We had only just arrived when a large black padlocked box was brought to the table, unlocked and tipped upside down with utter disrespect for the contents. Ballot papers swept across the table in all directions.

The guardian of the box then showed the inside of the box to the 'Indians' gathered at the table, sweeping his hand around the inside to show that it was completely empty. I found this quite exciting, having seen magicians perform a similar routine. Unfortunately the waiting audience was to be disappointed after he closed the box up. Not only did he fail to produce a pretty girl in a skimpy leotard, he even failed to elicit a measly white rabbit, instead leaving the box in the corner, forlorn and forgotten.

The council workers dived in like a pack of ravenous lions. Such an appetite for work surprised the uninitiated, who expected them to adopt their usual 'leaning on a spade' enthusiasm. That is if you did not know that, rather than an hourly rate, they were being paid a set rate for the job in hand, irrespective of how long the count took, or how quickly it was done. Doubtless it was this method of payment that animated the staff to an extent never seen in their lethargic toil at the council offices.

The first part of our poll was simply to count all of the voting slips to make sure that their total corresponded with the number torn out of the pads at the village hall. Had any of the Oakleigh electorate taken their voting slip and not put it into the box, one had the impression that the whole fabric of democracy would unravel.

Not that they stood much chance of escaping with a slip in Oakleigh; there were too few voters for anyone to slip past the 'guards'. However, it made one wonder whether larger electorates had security guards and bag searches on the way out, or one of those infernal machines they have in shops which announce to all and sundry if you have failed to pay for your goods, or in this case slipped a voting paper in your purse or pocket.

The voting slips were speedily put into bundles of 20. Each bundle was held together by that most humble, but invaluable, item of stationery, the paper clip. Then the bundles were stacked five high, each pile representing a hundred of those little crosses that we had sweated blood to obtain. It took a good twenty minutes just to make sure that the numbers tallied.

It was noticeable that some of the tables were surrounded by expectant supporters displaying their colours, while others remained aloof from the action: tranquil havens in a sea of party-political battlefields. The more marginal the seat, the greater the hullabaloo.

It was all quiet on the Oakleigh front. There were a few barely interested villagers brandishing their blue rosettes, and one solitary red beneath the vacant expression of an elderly lady who gave the impression of having fought one election too many. As I shook her hand she introduced herself as the Labour candidate, Doris Plummer. While I smiled at a fellow 'sufferer', Arthur scowled at my treason.

God-Leader-Election-Maestro Greenleaf was perturbed by the lack of many Conservatives at our table. It really seemed to have knocked some of the stuffing out of his confidence. He said that it showed the Tories thought that they had won.

I mused that with so many other elections being played out, ours could hardly expect to be Manchester United on Match of the Day. (The Oakleigh election seemed far more like a Grimchester United relegation game, and I was only on as a sub because the team was short of players.)

The count proper started with the ceremonial removal of the paper clips from each bundle. After this, the ballot papers were resprawled across the table in a haphazard fashion. The voting slips were then sorted into three piles according to the position of the cross on the paper. A filing tray marked 'doubtful votes' was centrally positioned on the table allowing the half-a-dozen counters to fling carelessly marked papers into it.

Arthur and Sally sat eagle-eyed but otherwise motionless on our side of the table, with nothing more than an abrupt "No!" should any of our voting slips finish up on the wrong pile. It would have been pleasant to record that this scrupulous display of honesty was extended, as a courtesy, to other names going onto my pile, but if the Greenleafs noticed any they retained a stony silence.

Doris Plummer, the Labour candidate, sat quietly, an enthusiastic smile crossing her face when the odd ballot paper went on her pile. One has to admire those who, whatever their political persuasion, persevere when they have as much chance of electoral success as they have of winning the lottery jackpot.

The few Conservative scrutineers initially sat impassively, showing little interest. However, as the piles grew, and it became obvious that the 'foregone conclusion' wasn't, they became more animated. They began to take a keener interest in making sure that they harvested all of their votes. As the count went on, more and more of the blue rosette tribe drifted over to the Oakleigh table, and their low murmuring indicated some disquiet.

Elsewhere the first results were coming in.

The deputy returning officer called the candidates and their agents to his table, and they whispered together as in a secret coven for several minutes before the result was announced in a slow lumbering manner. I couldn't decide whether this was his natural mode of speech, or whether it was an amateurish attempt to heighten a tension that had already been dissipated because the candidates already knew the 'score'. Even more importantly, if this was the wagon train's 'deputy' returning officer, then where was the sheriff?

The winning candidate would then make a short speech, thanking the staff and invariably launching into a diatribe against his beaten opponents or their party. This seemed particularly inappropriate and unsporting behaviour. Couldn't they simply shake hands with the losers, and leave it at that? Doubtless if Grimchester United have to play Liverpool, Manchester United, or Arsenal in the Cup next year, we will probably be hammered. I wouldn't like to see their manager on television rubbing salt in the wound by saying how badly we had played.

A hush fell over the assembled audience, many of whom knew what was about to happen. The deputy returning officer read out the votes cast, and announced a change of representation. The last Labour councillor in any of the villages had been unseated by the Conservatives. The Bluefoot Indians whooped for joy at having taken the scalp of a Redskin. Our count was three-quarters over. The Oakleigh Conservative candidate had still not arrived.

Long forgotten memories resurfaced of Saturday morning children's shows at the local cinema, where Indians would pat the palms of their hands across their mouths, and stamp their feet in a kind of war dance shuffle. (Come to think of it, that's where my dance style must have originated.) In their hands they would hold the golden hair of a scalped victim, although we all knew that it wouldn't be long before the hero gave them their come-uppance.

As my little piles of votes grew, I wondered whether I might be that hero.

CHAPTER SEVEN

FOR BETTER OR WORSE

With well over three-quarters of the votes tidied into piles, we had a slight lead, and I was beginning to wonder whether the Conservative candidate was going to show at all. Then he swept into the room in the style of a monarch into his state waiting room. One of his supporters quickly told him what was happening. Open handed, he advanced upon me with a genial smile but malice in his eyes. He shook hands with a perfunctory "So you're the Wuwal Pweservation chappie." Turning to his agent he seemed bemused.

"I can't understand what's gone wrong. Oakleigh has always been a safe seat. You told me so yourself. I shall be fwightfully annoyed if we do not win. It's weally not good enough. Whatever will they say when I am playing my next wubber at the bwidge club?"

The count continued. Occasionally Graeme Carstairs-Petherington would put on a spurt and take a slight lead, but he was rapidly overtaken every time by a certain John Edwards, and as we came to the final lap, Edwards lead grew ever greater.

Elsewhere in the gymnasium, counts were being finished and announced by the same man, who insisted upon reintroducing himself as the deputy returning officer, even though we were by now all fully aware of who he was. When each announcement was finished one sector of the audience, wearing uniform coloured rosettes would roar out their approval. The winning candidate would invariably amble to the microphone for his acceptance speech. These were hardly spontaneous affairs. Mostly it was a question of unfolding the paper from the inside of a jacket pocket and reading the contents. Just like a television cookery programme, the speeches featured an unspoken "here's one that I made earlier" spontaneity.

Awash with ballot papers.

A few of the defeated also insisted on making speeches, which was faintly embarrassing. It reminded one

of the kind of thing that the manager of Grimchester United might say on 'Match of the Day' at the end of a game in which they had been truly hammered. Not that Grimchester United have ever appeared on 'Match of the Day' you understand. For over 20 years, the 'Sardiners' have failed to reach even Round Three of the FA Cup, with its golden opportunity to play a major club and show television audiences those skills that, for a really good game have attracted league gates sometimes in excess of five-thousand supporters.

The thought struck me that the way that the count was going, I might soon have to make an acceptance speech myself. I made a careful mental note of what the other victors were saying, trying to get some meaningful ideas behind the smug and vainglorious rhetoric. I have to admit that the idea of speaking in public was one thing that I had not thought of, and it terrified me. However, a study of my predecessors onto the platform ensured that the idea became less intimidating. However experienced they might be as councillors, as public speakers most had little to offer.

Some spoke too close to the microphone, distorting the sound so that it was hardly intelligible. Some spoke so softly as to be inaudible above the cacophony of celebration. Speech impediments, boring monotone voices and a total lack of any attempt at humour; these all gave me hope that my own 'performance' would just slip by unnoticed.

The tiny piles of votes on our table were completed. The bundles of twenty slips had been piled five high, representing one hundred votes. I had four complete piles and a couple of loose ones. The Honourable Graeme Carstairs-Petherington had three complete piles and some loose bundles. Poor Doris was woefully short of even one fine high pile, having only just aspired to receiving a paper clip.

The head of the table waved a paper to the deputy returning officer as if it was a fan or a fly swat. This apparently indicated that the count was finished. 'Deputy' ambled over without even bothering to put on his gun belt. The head of the Oakleigh table showed him their tally and the little tray marked 'disputed votes'. The deputy returning officer then added up the figures. A glimmer of a smile and a certain tilt of the head gave relief to the staff at the table who now knew that their figures balanced, and that they would soon be able to go home.

'Deputy' called together the candidates and their agents. At his table we whispered together like plotting conspirators. The audience at a church sermon made more noise than us as we went through the figures. The result confirmed what we had already seen. We then turned to the 'doubtful votes'.

It doesn't actually take the brain of a mastermind to vote. When the voting slips says something like 'mark one name only with a cross' one would have thought that even the simplest electorate souls could master that without difficulty. Alas! Not so! Even that minuscule cerebral challenge proved too much for some of the residents of Oakleigh. The first slip that we examined had crossed out the names of my two opponents, so it was mutually agreed that the vote went to me. Three of the slips had ticks instead of crosses, so they were added to that candidate's pile of crosses. One voting paper was completely blank. 'Deputy' explained that what he usually did, with the candidates agreement, was to give such votes to the person with the least votes. We confirmed our willingness to follow precedence. Doris Plummer was particularly happy with this arrangement, it increased her vote by nearly 5 percent.

The final two papers were the most ambiguous, and resulted in the longest discussions. The first had put crosses next to my name and that of Doris, and a tick next to that of Graeme. Strictly speaking according to the instructions on the ballot paper, these should have represented half a vote each for Plummer and Edwards. However we conceded that the intention, if not the action, had been to vote for Carstairs-Petherington. Having conceded that vote to Graeme, he surrendered the last vote to me. This had three faces drawn on it, the artistic skill of which could have graced a nursery school, but not much further up the educational scale. Next to the names of Carstairs-Petherington and Plummer the face had a turned-down mouth, while next to mine the mouth had a smile. We assumed this to mean that the voter was happy with me, and dissatisfied with my opponents.

This manipulation of votes had been agreed very amicably, but I couldn't help but wonder whether the same courtesy would have happened had it been able to affect the final outcome. Just how good humoured would things have been had the disposal of doubtful votes affected the final result?

The pantomime cast assembled on stage for the finale of the Oakleigh Election Show under our own, our very own, Master of Ceremonies: 'Deputy'.

"I... David Thomas Stephenson... being the Deputy Returning Officer... do hereby declare that the total votes cast in this election to represent the constituency of... Oakleigh... on the District Council of... Sleepyvale... for the next four years is as follows...

"Carstairs-Petherington... Graeme Walter... The Conservative and Unionist Party... three hundred and sixty seven votes...

"Edwards... John Winston... The Campaign For Rural Advancement And Protection... four hundred and six votes...

"Plummer... Doris Agatha... The Labour Party... twenty two votes...

"And I hereby declare that the said... John Winston Edwards... is duly elected as Sleepyvale District Councillor for the constituency of Oakleigh."

There was a roar of approval from the tiny band of green and white, and green and black, rosettes. Even more surprising, their celebrations were supported by most of the other tribes of 'Indians' – especially the Redskins and the Multicoloured Alliance. Indeed, everybody seemed elated apart from the sombre Bluefoot who looked decidedly morose.

Suddenly I felt like a star! When the compere handed – oops! When the deputy returning officer handed me the microphone in the centre of the raised platform that acted as a stage, I had to suppress an overwhelming desire to burst into song. I did it 'My Way'; I won it 'My Way' comes to mind. Instead, I regained my composure enough to render a faltering off-the-cuff speech, very little of which I could remember even ten minutes later. I have a very vague recollection of thanking the deputy returning officer and his staff, having picked up that part of the speech from earlier winners. As for the rest? Well it was spoken from the heart rather than the head. I seem to remember pledging to work to the best of my ability for the villagers of Oakleigh. As for anything else only one other section comes to mind, and that for the wrong reason.

At some point in a bout of over-enthusiasm, I expressed my willingness to work with all other political parties for the benefit of the district generally, and my own village in particular. This had Arthur and some of his cohorts gnashing their teeth in disbelief, and shaking their heads vigorously in disagreement.

In my naiveté, I thought that a whip was when Jim, Greg and I put a fiver in a kitty at the pub. Only later was I to learn of another kind of whip whose job it was to tell councillors how to vote. Unfortunately for those so excited

79

at the prospect of another member of the party on the local council, I was to prove the most intractable of whipees.

One of the best things about being an election candidate is that you're not allowed to buy a round of drinks in the pub, in case it's construed as a bribe. This sounded like a great idea to me, especially since most of the regulars whom I see at the Pig and Crown were noticeably absent at the polling station. After all, they probably feel that a trip from the local hostelry to the village hall is fifteen minutes of wasted drinking time.

Unfortunately there is one major drawback to any alcoholic would-be-councillors. That is, whenever you have actually to fight an election instead of sitting back waiting for local party workers to present you with victory. Quite simply you have to work so hard that you don't have time for a good evening's drinking session. Now at last we had both the time and something to celebrate. But then, of course, the pubs were all closed.

I left centre stage to kiss and cuddle Penny, and to shake the congratulatory hands of Arthur, Sally, and the rest of our assembled party, apart from those still occupied in scrutinising votes elsewhere in Mudiford gymnasium. (Instead of a handshake, I wouldn't have minded giving Sally a kiss and hug as well, but stopped short not knowing whether this was the done thing.)

All the pubs might be closed, but thankfully my darling wife, being better organised, came to the rescue. 'Deputy' might not have been able to produce a rabbit from the ballot box, but Penny was able to magic a bottle of Sainsbury's finest champagne from out of a carrier bag that I hadn't even noticed her carrying.

Warmish champagne served in white waxed-paper cups isn't exactly how the films portray a celebration. But to us it was manna. Relief had come at last, at the end of a hard fought campaign. Victory had been secured in a fight that went to the finish. Elation combined with a glass of bubbly made me feel light-headed.

Hovering in the wings, was a tall, thin reporter from the Clarion dressed in a fawn mackintosh. Supposedly there to interview the defeated as well as new councillors, he took on the appearance of a praying mantis ready to strike at a moment's indiscretion from any of the assembled throng. As I started to giggle from tipsiness, he advanced upon me, notepad in hand.

It would be wonderful to report more overwhelming Party success in the elections, if there had been any. Shortly after the Oakleigh result, Councillor Mike Drinkwater was returned for Stepley, with an increased majority, but that was our only other win. We had candidates in a few other villages, but they all finished third or fourth. Whether this was due to the ability of the candidates, their opponents, or the lack of Arthur Greenleaf to steamroller though their villages I couldn't say.

Either due to an oversight on his part, or that of his parrot, Tom Renton, a streak of meanness, or the expectation of defeat, Mike did not provide any liquid refreshment.

We waited for the final result. This seemed a fairly pointless exercise, since the last seats were in urban areas where we didn't have any candidates. Besides which, the Conservatives already had outright control of the Council with a healthy majority.

At the end of the evening the political map of Sleepyvale was pretty complex. The total number of councillors was now as follows:

Conservatives 31
Labour 6
Liberals (Alliance) 2
Social Democrats (Alliance) 1

Social & Liberal Democrats 1
Social Democrats (non Alliance) 1
Liberals (non Alliance) 1
Campaign for Rural Advancement and Protection 2
Greens 1
Independents 2
Woodstoke By-Pass Action Group 1

Such complexities were too much for the local newspaper. Its coverage gave the result simply as:

Conservatives 31
Labour 6
Liberals & SDP 6
Others 6

It doesn't take a genius to work out that as long as the opposition was so diverse the Conservatives would have no problems in running the council how they wanted.

I was actually still not quite a councillor yet. On the Monday morning following the election, I duly presented myself at the Council Offices in Mudiford, shook hands with the Chief Executive and signed his big black ledger swearing allegiance to the Queen. Or was it to Sleepyvale District Council?

For better or worse, Oakleigh was now going to be stuck with me as their councillor for the next four years.

CHAPTER EIGHT

THE FIRST STEP ON THE ROAD
TO CHANGING THE WORLD

After the elation of the election victory, I had hoped for a bit of a rest. Such hopes were quickly dispelled.

On the Sunday morning following the election, I was summoned to a meeting of the full executive committee of Sleepyvale Campaign for Rural Advancement and Protection. Apparently, as a result of the confidence of the residents of Oakleigh, I had been instantly catapulted onto the full executive without even being aware of it. (Or even been consulted about a willingness to join, come to that.)

Expectations of a major meeting packed with people were quickly put right. There were just three of us in attendance. If this was the 'full' executive, how much smaller could the inner circle of the party be?

Mike Drinkwater and I, as the only District Councillors, were joined on the executive by the local party chairman, Tom Renton.

Tom took the chair and handed round agendas which read something like:

1. Election of District Council party leader
2. Election of District Council party deputy leader
3. Election of party spokespersons
4. Any other business.

Brian Rix would have been proud at the farce that was to unfold in the next couple of hours.

Tom kicked off.

"Item One. The election of a party leader for Sleepy-vale District Council. The leader must of course be a councillor. Are there any nominations?" After a pause in which nobody spoke he continued with: "I propose Councillor Mike Drinkwater. Have I a seconder?"

It didn't need a genius or a look around the room to see that I was the only one available.

"Seconded," I ventured a confirmation.

One might have thought that this would be the end of the matter, but Tom continued: "Are there any other nominations?"

Another pause ensued before, "All those in favour." Three hands shot up.

"I hereby declare that Councillor Drinkwater is elected as party leader on Sleepyvale District Council," confirmed Tom Renton.

Quite why we had to go through the stifling formality of Councillor This and Councillor That, instead of Mike, Tom or John, escapes me.

Since only councillors could take on leadership roles, the next move was even more farcical as there was only one person in the room now eligible to be deputy leader. Ordinary mortals may read in disbelief. However, one suspects that many local committee-type aficionados will be nodding their heads in remembrance of similar meetings.

"Are there any nominations for deputy party leader?" asked Tom without a shred of irony in his voice.

"I propose Councillor Edwards," suggested Mike helpfully.

"Seconded," added Tom. "All those in favour."

Two hands went up. Whether it was indecision about whether to take the post, or shell-shock at the rapidity of it all, mine stayed down.

On seeing this, Tom continued in his chairman role: "Against?"

Doubtless much to his relief, and that of Mike, my arm remained frozen rigid on the table.

The rest of the meeting followed a similar pattern. By the end of a very formal session, we had only ever used Councillor-Surname, without a single use of first names.

Mind you, I suppose that I shouldn't complain. I was now elevated from obscurity to be either party spokesman or deputy spokesman on every council committee. This included some, such as the TPOWP, that I didn't even know about.*♦

I had been looking forward to my first council meeting. It was the thrill of uncharted waters. It sated my ultimate ambition: running onto the pitch at Fish Park in a Grimchester United jersey, an opportunity that sadly had now passed me by.

As it was to become my second 'home' for many evenings in the forthcoming years, it would be a good idea to describe the council chamber in a little detail. It is a large rectangular room, with rows of high benches and seats along each side. At one end is a raised dais shorter in length, giving the impression of an altar. Behind this a very large crest is affixed to the wall: the coat of arms of Sleepyvale District Council all shining in gold, brass and brilliant colour.

On the opposite side to the crest is an area of open public seating, with a substantial wooden barrier between it and the rest of the chamber. Whether this is to protect councillors or members of the public from each other is not clear. Perhaps it's simply an innocent device to differ-

---

*♦(Authors Note: TPOWP. stands for Tree Preservation Order Working Party, who make the decision on which trees should have legal protection to stop developers knocking them down, etc. One of these would have been the best way of saving King Henry's 'Oak'.)

entiate between those allowed to take part in debate (councillors) and those who must just grind their teeth in rage and anguish without being able to say anything. The public area is stepped up, so that one is reminded of an audience at a dolphinarium, the councillors fulfilling the role of sea lions, without being anywhere near as entertaining. If a councillor barks to order and raises his flipper at the right time, perhaps he hopes that his leader-cum-keeper will throw him a fish.

The viewpoint of the Conservative ruling group tends to be well set out in our meeting agendas. After all, except when they are being specifically advised by senior council staff that what they are doing is wrong, much of the contents have invariably been prepared on their behalf.

The most interesting verbal comments therefore tend to come from leading opposition figures. Like the public, they sit at benches facing the prestigious Sleepyvale coat of arms. This design layout is very clever, since it means that the opposition have their back to the public gallery the whole time. This set-up makes it very difficult for Joe Public to hear what is being said. To help overcome this difficulty, and in the interests of fair play, a system of microphones on floppy wire stands are evenly spaced across all of the benches. These seem to have been manufactured by the same company that install loudspeakers at London railway stations. This gives councillors a stark choice: the option of speaking without mics so that many people can't hear them, or speaking with microphones so that the audience is aware that someone is speaking, but the sound is so muffled and distorted as to be unintelligible.

Now for the minutiae of the first full meeting of the new Council.

The various groups took their seats. The Conservative big guns took the high ground, their foot soldiers took the flanks. Labour took the centre opposite them, and the minor parties filled in on either side of the Socialists. The pro-and anti-Alliance elements of the Liberals and SDP tried to put as much distance as possible between each other. Likewise as the Green councillor sat in one corner, Mike steered me into the opposite corner. From this position we were virtually obscured both from the council chairman and from the general public. Quite a good position I thought. If the meeting was as boring as some of the televised so-called highlights of parliament, I could nod off without too much chance of anyone noticing.

The start was something of a surprise. We all stood up for the grand entry of a procession led by the present chairman of the council, closely followed by the chief executive and a man in a charcoal-grey suit wearing a dog collar.

The chairman opened with: "Good evening councillors. Please be seated."

He continued. "For our prayers this evening I have invited the Reverend Thomas Buckfast, Rector of St. Agnes Church, Tumblewell."

Instead of getting straight into the serious business of politics, I had somehow stumbled into a prayer meeting. As the cleric spoke, I mused whether all council meetings started like this, and in particular if the mayor or council chairman always chose the prayer-leader. As the current mayor of neighbouring Grimchester was a Muslim, how did they get on?

The reader may correctly surmise from these mental meanderings that religion does not feature centrally in my list of hobbies. The nearest I get to religion is a visit to the Grimchester United 'shrine' at Fish Park, and that only on alternate Saturdays during the winter months.

The clergyman prayed that we would all work together for the people of Sleepyvale, and that God would imbue us with wisdom – thoughts after my own heart. We all said the Lord's Prayer together, before the Rector's closing comments and disappearing act.

This brought back unpleasant memories of school assembly where a stern headmaster followed prayer by calling out the names of those he required to visit his study afterwards. When the name "Edwards, Class 4B" was read aloud, it wasn't for a pat on the back, but usually a meeting with the head's best friend and constant companion, 'Mr Whippy'.

Later council meetings were to prove that, despite the clergy's earnest intentions and the sincere participation of most of the assembled 'congregation', once the vicar had left, politicians felt free to go straight for each other's throats.

The first item of the agenda was the election of a new chairman for the forthcoming year.

"Are there any nominations?" asked the current chairman.

A man stood up from the middle of the Conservative ranks to speak.

"I nominate Councillor Albert Hepple," he said.

He then went on to elaborate for 20 minutes all of the fine virtues of his nominee, the outstanding work he had done for the community, the charities he had helped, etc.

To me, as a novice, this would have been very impressive had not the voice of Councillor Mike Drinkwater continually fed me a completely different opinion of the proposed chairman. "He's hopeless. He can't even follow the agenda. The other councillors constantly have to prompt him when it's time to vote. There's no way that he will ever be able to chair meetings." At the end of this extensive accolade, the chairman asked if there was anybody to second the proposal. Another keen Conservative bobbed up, a lady this time. She raked over all the same coals for a further ten minutes, as did Mike in my right ear. When she had finished, the chairman continued with the perennial question: "Are there any more nominations?" He was met by a stony silence. "I hereby declare that Councillor Albert Hepple is duly elected as Chairman of the District Councillor for the forthcoming year."

I had thought that Mike was exaggerating until I saw the new duly elected chairman being nudged by his neighbour to go up to the podium. He slowly rose to his feet and tottered up to the top table.

The outgoing chairman took off his chain of office, pinned it onto Albert's chest, and then helped the new chairman into his new seat. While the ex-chairman took charge of the miniature medallion that all of the other former chairmen wore, the chief executive handed Councillor Hepple a large black ledger.

Albert went to read from the book, then realised that he needed his reading glasses. He announced this to the chamber as he fumbled in his pocket for the right spectacles. This was met with sympathetic smiles from his Conservative allies, without a trace of irony, and by daggers from the more belligerent members of the opposition. I suppose that my own look could best be described as bemused by the whole affair.

After a good fumble, Councillor Hepple read out his oath in a quiet shaky voice. He then sat down relieved, as if his work was over.

The chief executive then leaned over and whispered something.

"Oh yes, I nearly forgot" came a faltering falsetto voice. "Can I have any nominations for vice chairman."

Albert's proposer popped up again. "I propose Councillor Mrs Hilyard as vice chairman."

He then unfolded several sheets of paper and we were treated to yet another anthology of her achievements. Thankfully this time there were no interruptions from Mike.

All there was from him was a kind of gentle refined deep breathing sound. I wondered if amid all of this gripping excitement, he had suddenly nodded off. However since he subsequently roused himself for the vote, I can only assume that he had closed down all of his systems and assumed a restful awakeness.

For anyone who had entered local politics to try to make the world a better place (in their eyes at least), they would surely be disappointed by the reality they faced.

Following the election of the vice chairperson, there was a thank you speech by one of her colleagues for the outgoing chairman and, even more bizarrely, a vote in support of the speech.

Then it was down to the distribution of seats on the relevant committees. Like much of the council work held in public, this had all been sorted out in advance. It was just as well since the whole unwieldy nature of the beast would have made things unworkable. Firstly each political group was allowed a total number of seats on all committees based on the number of elected councillors. Minor parties like ours didn't have enough 'points' to have someone on every committee, so the leaders sat down around a table and thrashed out on which committees they would be allocated seats. These discussions were fiercely fought out, particularly for seats on such committees as council policy and strategy, which by holding the purse strings could effectively overrule any important decisions by other committees.

Since the Conservatives were to take around two thirds of the seats on every committee, this fighting seemed irrelevant to me as an outsider. (Although now technically an 'insider', I still didn't yet feel a member of that inner circle that is local government.)

Finally the political leaders managed to agree the distribution of all of the seats among themselves. It didn't end there, however, because we still had to go through the motions of an open democracy. The procedure was now to elect all of the councillors into each committee in full council. This was a bit like the Football Association receiving each Saturdays' football results, reading them out at a press conference, and then voting on whether to accept them.

As the membership of each committee, sub committee, working party, etc. was agreed, the members of it all had to stand up for the election of a chairman and vice chairman. Since the Conservatives had a majority on every group, they had already agreed these posts beforehand. (Not that any of the other political groups felt inclined to nominate anyone from their own party anyway.)

Doubtless the system that we used has been closely studied and was the inspiration for thriving democracies around the world, like the recent state-controlled election in Albania (1987). Despite having an approved list of candidates, all from the same political party, turnout was 100%. The registered votes were 1,830,652 for the list, and one against. We didn't quite manage the one against ourselves.

The meeting went on for hours. Most of us did very little except bob up and down in our seats whenever there was an election involving a committee on which we were to serve. Just when I thought we had finished, there was another layer of elections – as representatives on outside bodies. And not just a few, but pages and pages of them.

By that time, I had lost any interest that I might have had in the differences between:

Sleepyvale Transport Strategy Executive

Sleepyvale Transport Consultation Group

Mudiford and District Community Transport Link

Sleepyvale Rail Users Consultative Committee

The Association of West Anglian Public Transport (Sleepyvale district)

Sleepyvale Bus Co-ordination Steering Group

and Grimchester and Sleepyvale Joint Transport Working Party

I just sat still and hoped that I wouldn't win any more elections.

CHAPTER NINE

FINDING A PATH THROUGH
THE MINEFIELDS OF POLITICS

Succeeding council meetings were considerably more constructive. In the smaller committee structure, every councillor had the opportunity to play a useful role.

Away from the politically poisoned fetters of Councillor Drinkwater, I felt able to contribute fully to the debate. My ego was suitably inflated by favourable comments from others when I said something particularly useful or astute. Doubtless this was due to the enormous benefit of innocence: having joined their club with no preconceptions and no hidden political agenda. In those early days, I made a point of listening to everything that was said. Thus I learned some particularly useful grains of wisdom that were to stand me in good stead throughout my term of office.

At home, like most 'committee-type' people, I am particularly well organised: to the point of being fussy. Likewise, on the council, I liked to 'label' my fellow councillors, using a system of cross-reference files.

The usual description of councillors relates to their political allegiance – Conservative, Labour, Liberal, etc. This is a very simplistic overview.

The Thatcherite Conservatives, in the ascendancy at this time, were in the majority and were represented by a pack of greedy money-grabbing wolves. Conversely, the most caring of all councillors (whatever their politics) was a sweet old Conservative lady who had been on the council for many years. She almost monopolised sympathy for the worse off. With a series of campaigns for crèches, the disabled, senior citizens, victim support and suchlike, she generally did more than anyone to help the vulnerable and underprivileged.

In their election literature, the Conservatives had made great noises about their financial acumen. You know the sort of thing, "Only we can manage the local economy, only we will use your money wisely; only we will increase services and at the same time cut your taxes, because of our financial expertise."

I was somewhat surprised therefore to find that they left financial matters almost entirely to the professional council staff to manage. Mind you, the best place for it I'd say. Still, the indisputable fact that many of them didn't seem to have even a basic understanding of budgets and accounts was a big surprise. Why did they keep beating the drum about their 'expertise' when it was so obviously lacking? How had they convinced so many of the general public about their financial fitness? I may support Grimchester United, but even if I kept saying that we were the only team worthy of winning the FA Cup, nobody would believe me.

Councillors who struggle to check the correct change when buying a newspaper are expected to deal with multi million pound budgets.

By contrast, the small Labour group, a political party allegedly infamous at the time for financial mismanagement at council level, had the only qualified accountant on the Council. At around six-foot-six-inches tall, he was not only physically head and shoulders above the legendary prudent Conservatives, he was also head and shoulders above them intellectually, taking a childish delight in running economic rings around them. The result was that whenever he rose to speak, his comments would be met by lots of rustling papers from the ruling party, as they desperately tried to find out what he was talking about.

This was by no means the only irony on the Council, for those who cared to seek it out. So, finally, I mention where it was spread most thickly on the other minor groups. These included an extremely militant Liberal, far and away the most intolerant (or il-Liberal) member of the Council. Meanwhile, the sole Green Councillor was a full-bearded individual who always wore old greasy patched jumpers and continually berated everyone in sight for not doing enough about pollution. One might have taken more notice of him had he not always sat down to resume smoking on his pipe, which smelt as though his baccy comprised rancid old socks soaked in diesel fuel.

Politics aside however, there were other criteria in my cerebral filing cabinets. Firstly there was the division between good, bad, and indifferent councillors.

The good councillors were those who actively pushed items forward, consulted local residents and generally galvanised the sometimes unwieldy council into action. The bad councillors were those who rarely attended, played little active role in council affairs and put in exaggerated claims for expenses. Between the two extremes was a solid core of mediocre councillors who usually turned up for meetings, rarely had much if anything to say, and needed prompting by their political leaders to remind them when and how to vote.

It didn't go unnoticed that the number of poor councillors increased, as a percentage, the larger the political party concerned. Not surprising really! If you won an election standing as a candidate for Marxist-Leninist-Revisionist or WASP Nationalist (White Anglo-Saxon Protestant), you would have to be dynamic and very committed.

Finally there was the division between urban and rural councillors. Left unchecked, the council seemed inclined to spend almost its entire budget on Mudiford and the other towns in Sleepyvale. That's where they put the sports centres, meeting rooms for the elderly and welfare groups, and of course the council offices themselves. It was in the towns where the Citizens Advice Bureaux were funded, housing estates spruced up, new children's playgrounds sited, and all the other elements that a council can use to make living somewhere a more pleasurable experience. We rural residents were left with...well, open fields around us and... not much else. I was therefore eager to join a cross-party lobby of some of the more active councillors in a sort of militant rural wing of the Council.

Finding my way around the council offices was a little more difficult. It was a veritable maze of corridors and small offices, with little plaques on each door giving obscure, coded, room reference numbers that didn't give a hint as to what part the people inside played in administering council affairs.

Finding my way around the maze of bureaucracy was even harder. Fortunately two avenues opened up with some success.

Ideas that were sensible, of general benefit to the residents, and didn't cost anything, could be bounced on the heads of some of the leading Conservatives. Since they controlled the Council, they could then claim the credit for any good ideas, even though their contribution may have been no more than to agree to support something in principle.

Whenever a bright idea needed some finance, an entirely different approach was needed. By going directly to the Council staff, and thrashing out ideas, one could have items anonymously appearing on the agenda, complete with costs, where the money was coming from and an endorsement by officers saying what a good idea it was. Of course if they didn't support an idea, it was effectively sunk in the water.

Council staff know that real power rests with them. Councillors tend to have an illusion that they are in complete control. The reality is that if the officers say a scheme won't work, but the Council push on with it anyway, the staff will make sure that it fails.

The one method to avoid like the plague is to bring an agenda item up proposed by such-and-such opposition group or member. This is the political equivalent of putting a notice on the back of your own jacket saying 'Kick me'.

Mike and Tom had assured me beforehand that the workload on the Council would be light. "Just a few short evening meetings a year." Mike and Tom are politicians, Politicians tell fibs when it suits their purpose. They must have seen 'gullible' written in large letters on my forehead. With the various committees, sub committees, working parties and outside representations, I was either in the Council chambers, or at another 'approved' meeting place elsewhere, for one or two evenings virtually every week.

Some of the so-called 'short' evening meetings started at seven o'clock, and went on beyond midnight. Although some of these were extremely important, a lot of the time it was a question of listening to the views of a lot of self-opinionated windbags who obviously thought that the rest of us didn't have anything better to do with our time. In addition, I was having to take an increasing amount of time off work, since it was only during the day that one could collar most of the council staff to go through detailed plans and ideas.

On the plus side, I found myself in receipt of a small sum from the Council to cover expenses in carrying out my duties. This brought a certain relief to my pocket, although the sums involved were certainly not sufficient to cover all of the costs that I was to incur during the year.

One of my close friends is a doctor. He keeps this a secret as far as possible. Otherwise, wherever he is, in the local pub, on a train or on holiday, he gets accosted by people seeking a free consultation. One supposes that they can't be bothered to queue up at the surgery, or maybe their problem is so trivial that it's only worth talking about when there is no effort involved in hunting the doctor down. After a few relaxing drinks, the last thing the good doctor probably wants is another alcohol-inspired, "'Ere you're a doctor; what do you think this is?"

In an effort better to serve the residents, I had arranged my own 'surgery'. Once a month in a classroom at the local junior school, Oakleigh residents could now pop in and see their district councillor to discuss – well more or less anything.

Of course I can't help everyone. About a third of the cases are services covered by the West Anglian County Council. I wrote to the councillor whose collection of villages included Oakleigh asking if she would like to improve the service available to villagers by sharing the surgery. Mike had been determinedly opposed to the idea of councillors from different political parties sharing the same surgery. In the event, it didn't matter. She didn't reply to my letter.

Another third of the services come from Oakleigh Parish Council. Again, I wrote to the chairman asking if one of the dozen or so Parish Councillors would like to join the surgery. At least he had the courtesy to reply. "Thanks. But no thanks." Basically as the parish councillors were non-political, they didn't want to be 'tainted' (my word, not his) by anyone in party politics. I was later to learn that there was just as fierce a political struggle on the Parish Council as on any of the 'higher' authorities. They simply preferred to fight without labels attached.

Needless to say, the letter that I wrote in my head, to our Member of Parliament, never got as far as getting onto paper, let alone meriting a stamp.

Apart from that, like my doctor friend, I keep my head well below the parapets. When I'm enjoying a quiet pint with Jim and Greg in the Pig and Crown, the last thing that I could possibly want is some stranger to find out my dark secret. Otherwise it would be a ceaseless parade of: 'You're on the Council. How much longer before...?', 'When are you going to do something about...?' etc.

Some people seem to believe that local councillors can do everything from improving their television reception to providing more Inter-City trains to places that I haven't even heard of.

As to council work itself. It can vary from absolutely fascinating to unbelievably boring. And all at the same meeting.

Belief that one can and will make a difference is a great motivator. But this is a painfully slow process. When running a marathon, the first step is the hardest. Well at least that's what you think until you actually run one, when you reach a point where each step becomes harder than the one before. Being a novice on the Council is a bit like trying to run a Marathon whilst immersed in treacle. I know that slowly I'm moving forward, but has anyone else noticed? Well at least Penny has noticed.

Nowadays, everyone seems to need a catchphrase. What's good enough for the famous is good enough for my wife also. Alongside Bruce Forsyth's "Nice to see you", Cilla Black's "Tarrah", and Michael Barrymore's "All-wight", can now be added Penny Edwards' immortal "Oh, not another council meeting."

I ought to be losing weight, as I'm getting into the Pig and Crown much less often. 'The usual' seems to be the empty glass of absenteeism. Then again, I suppose that playing pool or darts burns up more calories than languishing in the corner of the Council Chamber.

I serve on a variety of committees, trying to look intelligent when we get into technical discussions on various methods of ditch clearance, land drainage and suchlike. It has to be said that the vast majority of agenda items, for debate, hold little excitement, even for the participants. However do the members of the press keep awake?

Come to think of it, having read some of their reports, such as the regular 'Council Notebook' column in the Clarion, perhaps they had nodded off. They just seem to use the lively imagination of their dreams to conjure up a report. Many's the time that I've read a report in the newspaper, and had to look up whether I was at the meeting, so distorted is the article. Even I'm not that inattentive at meetings not to notice.

Insofar as this ramshackle collection of my memories as a councillor has any structure, here endeth the most mundane part. The bulk of a councillor's work may be important, but it hardly makes for riveting reading. The aim of this book is both to enlighten and entertain. Now that you have seen the perverse way that I, John Edwards, have been elevated to the Council, it would surely sorely try your patience to recount the minutiae of mundane meetings that occurred week after week. Instead perhaps some of the more amusing anecdotes, from my first year in of fice, may amuse you.

If not, you have my blessing take this book back to the bookshop from where you bought it. Simply say "I didn't enjoy this book. Please give me a refund in full." Then stand back – and watch the bookseller become abusive.

You may never get a straight answer from a politician, but the rest of the world is an entirely different matter.

Part Two

TALES OF THE UNELECTED

CHAPTER TEN

BROWN ENVELOPE SYNDROME

Having more or less won my way onto the Council through the preservation of a single rotting tree, one of my first challenges was to learn more about the mechanics that caused the situation to arise in the first place.

"One thing that I've never quite understood, Mike, is why nobody in Oakleigh seemed to have prior knowledge about the threat to our famous tree."

"Oh, I wouldn't say that, John," replied the experienced voice of Councillor Drinkwater, "Let me see – when the local plans were drawn up your councillor would have been..." He paused to think for a moment, "erm, of course, Phil Donnelly. 'Phil Mepockets' we used to call him; behind his back, of course. Yes, Phil was your District Councillor as well as Chairman of Oakleigh Parish Council."

"Ah yes, Phil Mepockets," added Tom 'the parrot' Renton.

"Well, why didn't he alert the village?" I asked somewhat naively.

"It doesn't take two and two to work that out. Phil was a damn good councillor. He was also a director of English Garden Homes plc, the largest housebuilder in the area and the parent company of the current developers. It wouldn't have been in his company's best interests to make too much of a song and dance about a nice piece of land that he'd already got his eye on."

"Not in his best interests" added Tom, emphasising

107

the 'his' and wagging his finger to emphasise the point.

"Goodness me, you don't mean...but surely that's corrupt?" I asked with incredulity.

"Oh no, it's perfectly legitimate," confided Mike. "Look, John, nearly half of the Sleepyvale Councillors are involved commercially in some way that benefits their company, a few directly, many more indirectly. Grimchester Councillors are the same. About a third of them are linked to the building trade in one way or another. You might almost say that they're sponsored by their companies. Look, how much time have you had to take off of work to go to important daytime meetings and the like?"

"Quite a lot already," I admitted, having been reminded of the fact on a number of occasions by my wife Penny.

"Well, let's take Portuguesa Sardines." Mike picked Grimchester's largest employer for his example.

"You work in a department like, erm, product development, for example. As a councillor, you are in an ideal position to keep the company abreast with what's going on locally that could affect them. Supposing they're looking for a new storage unit for their tinned sardines. As a councillor you're kept abreast of the latest voids; that is the number of units in the area that are empty. It's public knowledge, but pretty inaccessible unless you know where to look.

It's a bit like the local plans that you had so much trouble in finding. It might be a lot of hassle for Portuguesa Sardines to have to go through some long-winded process with a half-interested officer of the Council to find out the information they require. The answer is simple. Let your product development employee, who happens to be a councillor, supply you with the information.

Finding out that there are a lot of vacant units available, and that more and more leases are not being renewed could be very useful when Portuguesa Sardines actually start negotiating contracts with the Council. What does it cost the company? – a few days extra leave. What's in it for the employee-cum-councillor? Well, he gets a certain amount of recognition, important in a large company. It's in the company's interest to keep him sweet, with slightly faster-track promotion and the like.

I happen to know that any Grimchester or Sleepyvale councillors who work for Portuguesa are given fairly generous extra leave to do their council work. The company are actually quite proud of the fact, saying that they are helping the local community and enabling their staff to bring greater commercial awareness into the Council Chamber. You might almost say that Portuguesa Sardines are sponsoring some of the councillors."

I had nodded during Mike's comments, rather to show that I understood what he was saying, than that I agreed with him. On one issue, I remained morally outraged and continued to pursue the issue of the housing development in Oakleigh: "Surely you don't mean that you can buy a piece of land, and then pass it yourself for housing development."

"Nothing so crude, dear boy. The media's got it all wrong with their idea of brown envelopes stuffed with cash. Look, you work for a building company. You get advance notice from the District Planning Department of sites that are likely to be earmarked for development at some later date. You get your company to buy the land at a good price – more than it would be worth as agricultural land, but much less than its value as a housing development site. When the planning application goes through Council the application is already supported by the Council's own officers. You simply declare an interest, and receive a nice, fat bonus in your pay cheque. Simple and perfectly legal."

"I find all of this very difficult to believe" I commented.

"Look John, it's quite simple. Like yourself, almost everyone goes onto the Council for the best of reasons. But as a councillor you are privy to a vast quantity of useful material; in the right hands that is. You or I might not, but it's only human nature to make use of that information for self-betterment. Take my word for it, sooner or later, in one form or another, your temptation will come."

"It will come," added Tom, knowingly.

I returned home resolved to find a method of keeping the public better informed on planning issues, and to look actively for what I would consider other legal 'abuses' of the system.

In the meantime there was a more urgent matter that needed attention. I had to pore over the delights of the minutes of something called the Sport, Art and Culture Grants Working Party, on which I had somehow or other finished up as the party's representative.

The loves of my life, apart from my long-suffering wife Penny, are our two children – Arthur and Guinevere. (I have always had a keen interest in King Arthur and the Knights of the Round Table.) I would have liked more, but faced with the grim prospect of my wish to call any future son Lancelot, Penny hurried on down to a place called the Family Planning Clinic. I went with her the first time, and I cannot think of an institution with a more inappropriate name. Nobody there seemed to be planning a family.

As we sat in the waiting room, I surveyed our fellow consultees. Spotty girls barely a fortnight into teenagerhood, with breasts the size of walnuts, held the hands of thin anaemic boys scarcely older than Arthur. Alongside them sat Grimchester University Students with 'not awfully bright' written on their faces, and smart-suited career women who kept looking at their watches and occasionally held short, sharp conversations on mobile telephones. Then there were the young mums in romper suits, and bloated matrons whose distended stomachs showed that they had already finished planning their families. Men were few and far between, sitting nervously and watching the doors in dread anticipation of being seen by someone that they knew.

They were all there for the same reason as Penny and me – miraculous delights such as those tiny white pills that through the deepest mysteries of science stopped pregnancies. In the circumstances, Family Planning Clinic seemed a totally inappropriate name. Family Stopping Clinic or Postpone-a-Pregnancy would be far more accurate descriptions. I wonder if we could change the name? I must make a note to raise it a council meeting.

If Arthur was one of the loves of my life, then football was the love of his. If there was ever an England team elected on the basis of enthusiasm for the game, (their usually insipid lacklustre performance proves that they are not) rather than inherent ability, my son would have walked into the team.

Every waking moment when he was not being screwed down by his concerned parents to eat or study at table or desk, he could be found kicking a ball about. Our garage door was bent and dented from numerous practice shots, and the grassed area in front of our house was a bare patch of mud from numerous kickabouts.

He was good enough to make the squad of the local under 12s youth league team, Oakleigh Academicals, run by ex-professional footballer Georgie McCreadie. If you don't know the name, take heart. Even die-hard fans of Scottish League team Hamilton Academicals can barely remember a player of the same name who was bought for a pittance from Elgin City, spent one or two indifferent seasons in and out of their back four during one of their leaner years, and retired through ill-health brought on as a result of an overfondness for Glenturoch whisky. Otherwise he remains unknown, except in his adopted home of Oakleigh.

Being a member of the squad was certainly no guarantee of getting a game. It only signified the parents willingness to release their loved ones on a Tuesday evening for practice, and to pay the required £10 per year club membership as well as a match fee of £1.50 on days when one made that week's match team.

The undoubted soccer talents of Arthur, so patently obvious to his parents, seemed regularly to be overlooked by Georgie, since Arthur seldom even made the substitutes bench. We put this down not to any lack of footballing prowess by our son, but Arthur's inability to get his head around Georgie's overpowering Scottish accent, and the manager's poor judgement fuelled as it was by the Glenturoch. Our lad could have done anything asked of him on the football field, if he only understood what he was being asked to do.

One might have thought in the circumstances that we would take little Arthur away to a team able to recognise his brilliance, but he did still manage to play in the odd match: when the cubs and scouts went away for a weekend jamboree, or one week last January when nearly half of the regular team went down with influenza, Arthur stepped in to show everyone what a superb player he was. For some reason manager McCreadie always dropped him as soon as circumstance permitted.

Anyway as I pored over a list of dozens and dozens of applications for financial help from the many worthy organisations applying to next week's meeting of the Sport Art and Culture Grants Working Party, the telephone rang.

"Hello, John Edwards, how can I help?"

"Halo, it's Georgie McC-Creddy" came the reply, clicking half way through his name in a very unEnglish fashion. "Your bairn did well in practice last night. I thought maybe you would like to know that he'll be playin' with the first team this week."

"Oh thank you very much, Georgie," I replied, hoping that I had understood his challenging accent correctly, and surprised that he should have bothered to call.

"Don't thank me, man. It's no more than he is due. And if you continue to show your support for the team, then there's no reason why Arthur cannot play regularly."

So it was that on a cold and wet Saturday, while Penny was taking Guinevere to her ballet dancing lessons, I was stood on the touchline, supporting a proud Arthur.

If I were impartial, I would have to say that Arthur didn't seem to fit into the team as well as the grimfaced boy who usually played in his position, and who spent the entire match glaring with unrepentant fury at the cuckoo who had replaced him.

To give Arthur his due, he tried incredibly hard, running around the pitch like a demented fakir. The problem was that he saw very little possession of the ball. When he was able to get close to the action, his team-mates all seemed to look around desperately for someone else to pass to, other than Arthur. On a number of occasions they seemed to prefer to pass it to the opposition rather than our talented son. Eventually the game finished with Grimchester Youth Club Reserves winning by four goals to nil.

I did have a quick word with Eddie, to offer my condolences, but he would have none of it, insisting that it had been a good all round performance against one of the best teams in our division. I was even more surprised to hear that he thought Arthur had fitted in well.

Perhaps the clue to his new-found enthusiasm for playing our darling boy came in his closing remarks –

something about the club's grant application for new kit for the next season followed by: "I don't doubt that you will do your best by the club, you being a councillor and all that. Sure you support the team and there's no reason why Arthur cannot play every week. I could even see my way to giving him a wee bit of extra practice."

On the way home Arthur was really excited. "Oh" he said enthusiastically, "I'd give anything if I could play in the first team every week."

"So would I, son, so would I," I replied choking on my insincerity.

The following week we did indeed have to consider Oakleigh Academicals application for a grant for new kit, at the meeting of the Sport Art and Culture Grants Working Party.

**Anticipated bribery produced
a cuckoo for the soccer team.**

Anxious to do the right thing, I asked whether I had to
declare an interest in one of the applications because of my
son's involvement. Members of the committee found this
highly amusing, the great and the good themselves serving
on many of the organisations applying. Some of those pre-

sent had even filled in the application forms. It was patiently explained that I would only have to declare an interest and withdraw from the meeting if I was financially involved with the club, and in that respect £1.50 match fees were not relevant.

Opening the debate, the chairlady reminded the committee that we had received 187 applications for a total grants request of £242,000, (included in this figure was a certain request for £200 to pay for new kit for a certain youth soccer club) and that we had at our disposal the grand sum of £12,000.

"Because of this shortfall," she continued, "in previous years we have excluded localised grant applications, except where an individual or team were applying for grants to represent England at an international level. Instead, except in exceptional cases, we have chosen to concentrate on those applications that cover all or most of the district. Is it your wish that we continue that protocol this year?"

There was an undercurrent of murmured "ayes". I started to put up my hand to ask whether we could contribute towards my village youth team football shirts, then thought better of it, and remained silent.

Several hours later we had distributed nearly all of the money. Some was kept back as a contingency fund, for any late worthwhile causes. This was now my last chance to try to wrest some money for Oakleigh Academicals, but I blew it. Maybe I can console myself that having seen the local hospice and other charities receive only a fraction of what they had requested, mine seemed a fairly feeble cause.

I made my way despondently home wondering how I was going to tell my son that his dad had caused him to be dropped from the soccer team. I wondered if I volunteered to make a large personal contribution towards new team

shirts, Arthur might keep his place. That would be a first –
the councillor having to hand over his own cash in a
brown paper envelope.

I'm pretty lousy at this corruption lark. Let's hope I
make a better councillor.

CHAPTER ELEVEN

*THE TRUTH, THE WHOLE TRUTH AND AS LITTLE OF
THE TRUTH AS ONE CAN GET AWAY WITH*

For a few weeks after the election a number of people are
able to remember the names of their councillors. As the
passage of time passes the number who know declines, until after four years, when the time comes for re-election,
you are almost completely forgotten, except by a few
hardened enemies whom you have managed to upset. You
know the kind of thing: those where you wouldn't support
their planning application to extend their semi-detached to
five storeys high, or where you were unable to stop a couple of ten-year-old boys kicking a ball about on the ex-
panse of green open space in front of their houses.

So at the beginning, when the name was still fresh in
people's minds, I was invited by the headteacher of Mudiford Comprehensive to speak to his Sixth Form General
Studies students. Enthusiasm in my new-found fame completely distorted a common sense refusal, and I agreed to
meet and discuss the idea with the headteacher, a Mr Arkwright.

To say that my experiences at school were happy
would be a blatant lie. We used to nickname our teachers
according to their personal traits – Atilla the Hun, Ivan the
Terrible, Vlad the Impaler, and that was just the ones dis-
liked the least.

Mr Arkwright, who insisted that I call him David, was
a charming man, quite handsome, probably under 40 years

of age, and with an affability that was contagious to his pupils. In the corner of his office, I spied neither cane, birch, nor cat o' nine tails on display, no hidden rack, or thumbscrew, or any of the other imaginary devices of torture with which headmasters intimidated pupils when I was at school. Perhaps it is something to do with de-sexing them that has turned them into human beings. Headmasters and Headmistresses left one with the impression that they had chosen a career as professional sadists. After all, sadists refer to themselves as Masters and Mistresses. How much more evil must a HEAD Master or HEAD Mistress be? Head Teachers on the other hand, seemed merely the first among equals, able to chat amiably to the students.

Anyway, David briefly explained the kind of subjects that would be suitable broth for his A-level studies group.

(For those unfamiliar with A-level General Studies, it's about nothing in particular, and is recognised by virtually no Universities, except some of the newer converts such as Grimchester University. Formerly a very mediocre technical college, this is now an even more undistinguished University.)

I went away full of enthusiasm for the idea of a lecture, rather than full of ideas for a lecture, and this problem became more acute as the time for the lecture approached. Then, whilst reading a copy of the Grimchester and Sleepyvale Clarion, I was inspired by the front page, although the article itself would hardly seem suitable fodder.

GRIMCHESTER COUNCILLOR IN SEX SCANDAL

**The councillor insisted
that he was on a fact-finding mission.**

Councillor Ken Brimshaw's car has been recorded three times in the past month kerb crawling in the city's red light district.

Councillor Brimshaw, who has represented Grimchester Gasworks ward for Labour since 1972, has been reported by the Police to the Crown Prosecution Service. A spokesman for the Crime Prosecution Service. declined to answer questions from your *Clarion* crime reporter.

Councillor Brimshaw has emphatically denied any wrong doing, claiming that he was looking into local social problems created by the town's working girls.

When challenged by *The Clarion* that we had spoken to some of the girls, and that he had discussed prices for a range of services, he insisted that he was surveying the degradation to which they would stoop, and the amount of money that they could earn in an evening.

He felt that it was wrong that the Exchequer was losing so much potential income tax, and was very worried that some of the girls may also have been defrauding Social Security by claiming to be unemployed.

Councillor Brimshaw laid the blame for the situation squarely at the door of the Prime Minister.

He stated: "The actions of Margaret Thatcher in creating widespread poverty and unemployment has forced decent, ordinary girls to work the streets. They are victims of her vicious policies, and I am now being persecuted by her police force for trying to reveal the full extent of the problem."

Since our discussions with Councillor Brimshaw, we have discovered from his local newsagent that Councillor Brimshaw has *Rubber Mac Review in Colour* and *Bondage Monthly*, in addition to your favourite newspaper, *The Clarion*.

We telephoned Councillor Brimshaw's office several times to ask him about the latest developments, but he was always unavailable.'

Of course, Councillor Brimshaw's activities, innocent or not, would in no way be incorporated into my talk. Rather, it was his apparent inept deviousness which inspired it. I therefore sat down and began scribbling – a monumental speech, that would be both down-to-earth and uplifting, on the merits of being open, honest and truthful.

We all have skeletons in our cupboards that we would prefer never to see the light of day. I'm sure that *The Clarion* would love to get hold of the real story of a certain newly-elected Oakleigh District Councillor's activities on his company's four-day team-building and employee-bonding break in Torquay last summer.

The bonding sessions between the aforementioned councillor and his secretary, Dilys, were certainly not on the official curriculum. A surfeit of wine and after dinner brandy, and the balmy English Riviera in June were our excuses for a romantic evening followed by a hot and sticky night with a very pleasurable exchange of body fluids. Deliciously exciting as it was at the time, we were both considerably embarrassed about it in each others company for months afterwards. I certainly wouldn't want my wife Penny to find out about it, and the thought of it being splashed all over the newspapers positively sent cold shivers down my spine.

However, sympathy for the plight of Councillor Brimshaw's predicament would in no way jeopardise my speech which, because of the audience for whom it was intended, had to be full of lofty ideals on truth.

The following evening I had just finished putting the finishing touches to my masterpiece when the telephone rang.

"Oakleigh 3605."

"Is that the councillor?" asked a squeaky female voice at the other end of the line.

"Yes, this is Councillor Edwards. How can I help?"

"Oh, erm... this is Mrs Betty Barnwood of 14 Foxglove Close... It's about my neighbours... They've got rats in their garden."

"I see, and have you spoken to them about it?"

"Oh no... I don't think that I could do that," replied Mrs Squeaky Voice.

"Well in that case," I continued, "perhaps you would like to telephone the environmental health department at the Council, so that they can send an officer around to investigate."

"Done that," she replied. "They said they couldn't help."

"I'm surprised at that," I consoled. "Perhaps I could come and discuss it with you. Would it be convenient if I came round and saw you now?"

Ten minutes later, I was being invited into the lounge-diner of a neat matchbox that claimed the address of 14 Foxglove Close. After I had been comfortably seated with a cup of tea, our conversation turned to rats.

"So what exactly did the Council say?" I started up the conversation.

"Well...they said that they couldn't find any evidence of rats...but it stands to reason, doesn't it?...I mean...well, you know."

I have to say that at that moment I hadn't the faintest clue what Mrs Barnwood was talking about, and I had to politely tell her so.

"Well... there's got to be rats there... I've seen the grass rustling... and now that we've got some of T.H.E.M. next door... well it stands to reason."

T.H.E.M.? Oh, some of them!?" hoping that she understood the quizzical tone of my voice, while wondering whether rat-breeders, new age travellers or Martians had invaded Oakleigh, or whether the dear lady was simply a bit dotty.

"Yes... you know..." and her voice lowered to a whisper, "Pakis."

"Oh, I see," and indeed I had begun to see that Mrs Barnwood's suspicions about rats were really suspicions about her neighbours.

She continued: "Before we know it...we'll be overrun with them."

"What Pakis?" I asked somewhat naively.

"Well them... and rats too! Not that I would want you to think that I was... well... you know... racist."

I smiled a reassurance, wondering if she saw any trace of sarcasm on my lips or in my eyes.

"Well, they've only got two children at the moment... but you know how fast they breed... Maybe they've eaten some of their own babies already... so we won't get suspicious... Before you know it... well... they'll have taken over the village."

I have never quite understood why so many seemingly good people seem to think that other cultures like to eat babies. I remember quite recently a priest on television who genuinely believed that Russian Communists were eating their own children, and no doubt there are commissars in the Soviet Union preaching that rich Western capitalists feast on the babies of the poor down-trodden workers.

"Why don't they go back where they come from?" she continued.

"Grimchester?" I ventured, trying to inject some playful humour, knowing that there was almost every nation under the sun within that town's limits, and this was the most likely last port of call for the neighbours.

"No," she said, reacting as if she was speaking to an idiot: "India...where all the Pakis come from originally."

I considered whether to enlighten the good lady that 'Pakis' come from Paki-stan, rather than India, but she was only using the term as a generic word-peg on which to hang anyone with brown skin.

"Would it help if I went and spoke to them?" I enquired.

124

"Would you mind... I would feel better if I knew what they were up to... I'm a good Christian, you know... and I don't want... you know," and she reverted to a whisper again, "devil-worshippers on my doorstep."

I left wondering how many good Christians, if they had been fortunate enough to see Christ in the flesh, with his weather-beaten brown skin, black hair and Semitic appearance, would call him a 'Paki'.

I wasn't quite sure what to expect when I knocked at number sixteen, the home of Mr Rugundo. A short, balding, slightly tubby man dressed in casual shirt and slacks opened the door, his skin not much darker than mine when I get back from my annual two-week pilgrimage to the Sun God. (I usually find him available for worship during the month of August in Majorca or on the Spanish mainland coast.)

"Hello, I'm sorry to trouble you. I'm your District Councillor, John Edwards." I held out a hand and my warmest smile.

"Ah, so you have about the rats, I suppose?" his reply was immediate, relaxed and very matter-of-fact, as if he was fully expecting a visit. The accent was distinctive – middle English with an undercurrent of South Asia overlaid with a trace of the Grimchester twang.

"Well yes, I have had a report that you might have had a rat in your garden," I volunteered.

He broke into a broad smile. "Please come in," he beamed, and took me into a comfortably appointed lounge, which was a replica of the one next door, except that the furniture was newer and more stylish, and the decor brighter making the small room seem more spacious.

"This is my wife Sunita."

I took the hand of a slightly rotund lady whom I had expected to be in a sari, but was actually dressed in a plain green dress with white collar and cuffs of the sort readily available in C&A or M&S.

"Hello, John Edwards... local councillor."

"Would you like some tea, Mr Edwards?" she asked, being hospitable.

"Yes, thank you, and please call me John." I suddenly thought that perhaps I was being a little forward exchanging Christian names with an Eastern lady, until I remembered that Mr Rugundo had introduced her by her forename.

"Assam, Earl Grey or Darjeeling?"

"Whatever you are having will be fine" I replied, being unsure what 'breed' of tea leaves went into PG Tips.

After tea and polite conversation about what Mr Rugundo insisted on calling his 'lovely English village', we got down to the business of the supposed rats. I proceeded to explain that there had been a suspected sighting of a rat rustling in the grass.

"Perhaps you would like to come into the garden to see for yourself?" he enquired, and we decamped into a small nondescript area comprising a tiny lawn with a few sickly looking shrubs that the builder had probably called a landscaped garden when he had sold the property.

On the lawn were two small children, aged about ten or twelve, playing with a light-grey kitten.

Mr Rugundo laughed, "I expect that one of my neighbours glimpsed the children's kitten, and thought that I was one of those lower caste Asians from Grimchester Old Town, and had imported rodents into the village. The Council inspector has already been to see us. He couldn't find any trace of a rat, unless of course" and here he broke into a mischievous smile "we have already eaten it."

"Well thank you, Mr Rugundo, I'm sorry to have taken up so much of your time."

"Not at all, not at all, and it is Doctor Rugundo. We haven't met many people here yet as we've not been in the house for very long. It is always a pleasure to meet with people like yourself who have a high standing in the community."

"Oh, I'm sorry, I didn't realise. Is that a doctor of medicine?"

"Yes, of course, although I can understand why you needed to ask. We Govindrans hold doctorates in many subjects."

"Govindrans?" I ventured.

"Yes. Govindrans are a separate race and religion. You may not know of us much in the West, but we are renowned throughout the Indian sub continent as the most cultured of races. We provide the greatest scientists, doctors and mathematicians. Our poets and writers, composers and musicians are the finest in Asia. Our religion is unique. Although it is a branch of Hinduism, it takes the best elements from all of the great religions of the world – Jainism, Buddhism, Islam, Zoroasterism, even Christianity – to create the Great Universal Truth. Just as Latin used to be a sign of culture in Europe, so, in Mother India, simply being able to speak Govindran is the highest intellectual achievement that one can attain."

"Well thank you again. I've learned a great deal. I hope that you will be happy in our village."

"Thank you for welcoming us," he replied, and we shook hands as we parted.

I'm not quite sure where the expression 'strike while the iron's hot' originated, but I went straight back to Mrs Barnwood.

"Hello, Mrs Barnwood. Well, I've been to see your neighbours, and saw no sign of any rats. Doctor Rugundo thinks you probably saw the children's kitten."

On hearing the word 'doctor', Betty Barnwood's entire demeanour changed. "Oh, a doctor!…Oh that's all right then…I had a lovely Indian doctor when I went into hospital to have my haemorrhoids done…Thank you very much…erm…you know…for putting my mind at rest."

I suppose that you would say smug was the expression on my face, as I returned home to complete my speech.

Two days later, on the eve of my speech to the Mudiford Comprehensive Sixth Formers, there was a knock on my door, which opened to reveal Doctor Rugundo. I invited him in for a cup of PG Tips.

"I'm very pleased with your help," he said. "Mrs Barnwood came around yesterday and brought us a home-made sid cake, and my wife Sunita is going to show her how to make a Govindran Chicken Curry tomorrow. Govindran Chicken Curry is the finest curry in India; well come to that, it's the finest curry in the entire world."

"I'm pleased things have worked out so well, although I haven't got a clue what sid cake is."

"It is like your fruit cake, but with sids in it."

"Sids? Oh, you mean seeds; it's seed cake" I replied.

Doctor Rugundo looked confused. "That is what I was telling you – sid cake." He pulled from his pocket a small leather pouch. "I would consider it an honour if you would accept a little token of my esteem." He handed me the pouch

"Thank you, you really needn't have."

I peeked inside, intrigued by the contents. Perhaps it was one of those exotic sounding teas, although it didn't smell like any tea that I knew.

Seeing my bemused look, Doctor Rugundo enlightened me. "It is made from the finest ingredients – a secret recipe of Govindran herbs supplemented with dried flakes of Afghan stallion testicles, and a tiny pinch of ground tiger bone. It is a very good tonic for pleasing the wife. If you are ever having a little trouble holding your erection, well to use an English expression – it will put graphite in your pencil."

"Well thank you. By the way the expression is to put lead in your pencil."

"Oh no, sir. You would not want to put lead in. It is a heavy metal, and highly poisonous to the system. This is a fact that has been known to Govindran medicine for thousands of years, even though the West has only realised it recently."

"Well, thank you, anyway. I must say that these are somewhat unusual ingredients for a doctor to prescribe," I commented.

"For a Western doctor of medicine perhaps. For a doctor of Govindran medicine, these are some of the traditional remedies that we use. I know all of the herbs, the fungi and the plants, to treat all forms of disease from the common cold or influenza to warding off the evil eye or possession by demons. Although I am a qualified doctor of Western medicine, I have not forgotten our traditional herbal remedies. One day, in the not too distant future, I believe that the West will realise that there are alternative medicines just as effective as today's processed drugs."

After the good doctor had gone, I sat down to ponder whether Mrs Barnwood would want to know 'the truth, the whole truth, and nothing but the truth'. Having satisfied myself that she wouldn't, or perhaps more accurately that the knowledge would only mean more difficult times ahead for the local councillor, easily settled the matter.

Instead I put Doctor Rugundo's little leather pouch in our souvenir display cabinet between a Spanish flamenco doll and a donkey with a straw hat, and contemplated tomorrow's speech to the A level General Studies students. This need to surpress the truth had put me in a dilemma. Could I get away with minor tweaking, or would I have to completely rewrite my speech to the students? Indeed was there any way that I could make the speech convincing, in the light of my latest personal experiences. Only the General Studies class of Mudiford Comprehensive School know, and they are far too busy revising, for their more important A level subjects, to tell you.

CHAPTER TWELVE

AN UNFORTUNATE TIME TO DIE, THE LAST BASTION
OF THE CLOTH CAP, AND A SURPRISING NEW
START

When the Council leaders had been distributing seats on
the various committees, Mike Drinkwater had been very
careful to ensure that we didn't have a representative on
the housing committee.

He had explained that the committee was a lot of hassle with little electoral reward for us. Since, like most other
facilities, the majority of the council houses were in the
towns, this seemed pretty sensible. Oakleigh only has two
blocks of council houses totalling only a dozen terraced
houses, albeit with longer gardens than many of the nearby
private dwellings.

This opt-out decision was warmly welcomed by both
Labour and the Alliance of Liberals and Social Democrats
who saw this as a battleground in which to fight for the
dubious pleasure of leading the opposition. They were
only fighting for the political crumbs offered by that worthy organisation, responsible as it was for the administration of all the council houses. The Conservatives, who still
retained overall numerical superiority, seemed to regard it
with little interest, except as a troublesome source of possible income.

One of the big advantages of our opt-out arrangement
should have been that I only had to worry about the problems of a handful of tenants. Unfortunately it didn't quite

work out like that. There were always too many suitable applicants desperately trying to get into the village in one of the too few council houses.

It is very difficult not to have sympathy for life's less fortunate, and certainly the plight of many of those trying to get a too-rare council house fell into that category. In my experience, the overwhelming majority of them were very decent people who, for one reason or another, were simply poor. I have found some of them to be the most generous of people but less well equipped to deal with the realities of the rat race. I'm sure that the desire to help these people is a major cause of why some of mankind's more intelligent and successful give up so much of their free time to become councillors. One assumes the higher orders of politicians must be likewise driven.

Unfortunately a few of the council tenants, whom many would regard as losers, actually did very well for themselves. These were the professional 'spongers'. They didn't usually work, at least not officially. They continually pleaded abject poverty, and how hard done by they were. Nevertheless they seemed genetically programmed to know how to milk the system. They certainly seemed to have no problem acquiring the necessary resources to consume large quantities of beer and fags on their so-called pittance, and the satellite dish on their outside wall was a cost too far for many a home-owning worker.

One of the saddest housing cases I had to deal with was that of a widow whose recent dear departed husband had been a regular at the Pig and Crown. Dave Gear was as much a fixture in the Pig and Crown public house as the pump handles, lights and furniture. It was difficult to remember a time when he wasn't sat in 'his' chair in 'his' corner. He was always dressed in the same raincoat, and a flat cap was a permanent fixture on top of his head.

When he got up, it was only to order another pint of draught Barron's Old Redoubtable, one of the pub's speciality beer barrels. Cast-iron bladder, summer and winter, rain and shine, there he sat, pint in hand, chatting to some of the semi-regulars whom he called friends. With them or without them, the Racing Post was invariably opened in front of him, and in quieter moments he would be drawing strange symbols to indicate the chance of various race-horses winning or placing. No archaeologist studied the Dead Sea Scrolls so intently, or for so long, as Dave Gear studied his newspaper.

Then one day he was not there. A couple of weeks later I received my monthly council update of the electoral roll. This informed me that Dave Gear had moved on to the Great Saloon Bar in the sky. He was no more than a passing acquaintance, but it's always a jolt to one's own mortality when somebody you know dies.

The departure from this life by this particular Pig and Crown regular was soon more or less forgotten by most of those who drank there. However, a few months later I was to receive a reminder when his widow contacted me. Somehow the thought of Dave having a life outside of the pub had escaped me.

I went to see Gladys Gear at her tiny early nineteenth-century mid-terraced cottage near the centre of the village. The house looked abandoned. A few patches of peeling paint still obstinately clung on to woodwork otherwise devoid of decoration. One didn't have to be a builder to note the windows rotted almost to extinction, the cracked panes, the twisted chimney and missing slates. No chance that this house would pass an MOT.

Gladys was tiny, both in height and frame Her face was lined by the ravages of years of hardship, hard work and worry. She looked so much more frail than her husband Dave, who had looked the picture of ruddy health up until the time I had last seen him.

She invited me into her living room, which had a front door opening onto the street, and was made even smaller by the staircase in it. We crossed thin threadbare carpets to sit on a small well-worn shiny settee. I opted for tea (hoping that she could spare a T bag, and that she would squeeze two cuppas out of it). I was served mine in a pretty white bone-china cup with painted flowers on it, and a matching saucer. The particular shape with its tiny ornate handle had been popular fifty years or so earlier. Gladys herself drank from a nondescript coarse-looking yellow cup with a mis-matched saucer. I made a mental note to try not to break what was probably her last 'best' cup and saucer.

The tale that Gladys told me in her soft fragile voice was one of a wasted life, although she told it in all its fantastic detail without a trace of bitterness. Her husband had been addicted to gambling on the horses which was every bit as financially draining as his fondness for Barron's Old Redoubtable. Although he had a very well-paid job, his twin distractions had reduced them to a state of permanent poverty. Their only child, a son, had been killed in the Korean War. Although a similar story may be told in many other homes throughout the country, it was the peculiar nature of Dave Gear's last will and testament that made their case unique and bizarre.

It appeared that in keeping with several of his fellow-punters, he liked to follow and bet on particular horses. He would study current form, the jockey, the going, etc. As a consequence some weeks he would come home with several hundred pounds in his pockets. On these occasions he would give Gladys an extra five or ten pounds "to buy yourself something nice". Unfortunately most weeks he came home with an almost empty wallet, frequently having to raid the biscuit barrel, where Gladys kept her housekeeping money, for just enough emergency cash to pay for a glass or two of liquid refreshment at the Pig and Crown. Gladys, whose father had been similarly minded with her mother, found this arrangement perfectly natural. She admitted to gently chiding him only very occasionally, which he apparently took with good humour.

In his will, Dave had wanted to make amends for the

poor life that Gladys had led. He wanted her to have every comfort in her twilight years. Unfortunately he remained ever the optimistic gambler right to the end. His instructions were that his entire estate, including the house where they lived, be bet upon a particular horse in its first available race. The solicitor advised Gladys that the current choice of nag had been the fifth such nominated horse. Dave had kept the same will throughout and used codicils to amend the name of the animal selected, as the form of each favoured horse ebbed and flowed. Appropriately enough the current, dubious, four-legged beneficiary was named 'Glad All Right'.

Somehow Dave had convinced himself that should he be unlucky enough to die, his bad luck would be translated to good fortune on the race track. In this sense he was no different to many other people who think that there is some higher being that ensures an equality of fortune: the twin gods of Destiny and Fate working together so that everyone gets their fair share of good luck.

Somehow Dave appeared to have utterly convinced himself about this innate balance to life. With his demise, having deprived his wife all of her life, his dearest wish was to see her live out her old age in relative prosperity. Doubtless he died thinking he would succeed.

Gladys Gear's solicitor, who told her that he had very reluctantly drawn up Dave's will, had advised her that she could challenge the intention, through the courts if she wished. He was confident that the stipulation could be easily overturned. Of course, he had not been so reluctant about the will as to refuse to draw it up. If one was cynical, it could be said that this mischievous clause and the ensuing codicils were a guarantee of further employment for him.

In her charming, if witless, way, Gladys declined the advice. Rightly or wrongly, she had always stood by her husband's decisions and would continue to do so to the end.

An unusual arrangement was made with a major chain of turf accountants to value the house, and to put the value of it into an account for Gladys. There the sum of money was joined by some trifling amounts from a small life insurance policy and the residue of Dave's savings after the funeral costs had been met.

Some of Dave's friends helped Gladys to keep an eye out for the prodigal horse, and in due course Glad All Right appeared in the list of runners, appropriately enough in the Portuguesa Sardines Handicap, run over seven furlongs. This was a little further than usual for the horse who invariably ran over five or six furlongs. However, Dave's friends were hopeful that the selected horse had acquired additional stamina with the passage of time.

On race day, Dave's 'expert' friends were more concerned with rain than racing. It had been raining fairly steadily for two days, and Glad All Right liked firm going, where speed could triumph over stamina.

In a large field 'Glad All Right' was second favourite at five-to-one. If Dave Gear's premonition was right, Gladys stood to inherit a tidy sum, certainly more than she had ever seen in her life. However, Dave's friends were clearly worried with so much at stake. They advised her to wait for another race, when the going wasn't so soft, or the distance was shorter. They tried to persuade her that it was what Dave would have done himself. But Gladys was adamant in her resolve. The bet would go on.

Dave's friends tried one last idea. They urged her to back Glad All Right both ways as conditions didn't favour it. With so many horses, the bookies would be paying out for the first four finishers. Glad All Right might not be good enough to win on the day, but it would surely make one of the places. Again Gladys declined the advice. She insisted on putting everything on to win, as Dave had stipulated.

For the first and only time in her life, Gladys entered one of the last bastions of male dominance: the betting shop. One of David's closest friends took her in and showed her how to fill in a betting slip. As he took her through the hazy blue smoky atmosphere to the counter, almost none of the other customers noticed that rarity – a woman in their midst. Women weren't actually banned from coming in, but rarely did so, except for a day or two leading up to the Grand National. Of course, the punters were so intently poring over the newspapers on display, or watching the poor quality television in the corner, that they hardly noticed her.

The clerk did. When the slip was handed over, his mouth dropped in disbelief. Then he had to disappear out the back to check with the manager that this poor-looking frail lady did indeed have over £40,000 available in her account to put on a single race.

Gladys confided that the clientele reminded her of those Jarrow marchers that she had watched on the cinema newsreel when she was a child. Until then, she didn't realise how many people this far south, other than her late husband, still wore cloth caps.

Gladys returned home and switched on the television. Doubtless she could have done with a stiff drink by her side.

They were off!

Glad All Right went into an immediate lead, and by halfway the cherished beast was three lengths clear of the rest of the field. It continued to run on, still with a clear lead from the chasing pack with just a furlong left to run.

One can only wonder at the excitement of Gladys at this point, with her horse clear, and close to a quarter of a million pounds beckoning. Maybe she even glimpsed her late husband's fatal fascination for the sport of kings.

But the thin bony finger of Fate is fickle.

The rest of the horses pressed home. Glad All Right didn't tire noticeably, but in the heavy going it simply couldn't up its pace. In less than a minute, Gladys saw her small fortune melt away, as one by one other horse outsprinted Glad All Right on the run-in. Glad All Right came in fifth.

Doubtless had she'd the foresight to have a strong drink by her side, Gladys Gear would have taken a large slug from the glass. I certainly would have.

Gladys was ruined. The race had confirmed her original opinion: gambling was a mug's game. Perhaps it even tarnished her own seemingly unshakeable faith in her dear departed husband.

So how did I come to be involved in her sorry tale? With the sale of her house, Gladys was not only destitute, but homeless. The turf accountants were more generous than they needed to be, giving her three months notice to quit. Three months may seem like a long time, but time has its own relativity. The older one gets, the faster it goes. To a poor old lady a month passes as fast as a day to a child. Not that Gladys was inactive, you understand. She immediately contacted the housing department of Sleepyvale District Council asking their help in finding somewhere else to live in Oakleigh.

The Council's response was fairly negative to say the least. With houses in such short supply, they hid behind the defence that Gladys had made herself intentionally homeless because she had not challenged Dave's will. At that point, she turned to me for help.

The extent to which councillors can influence housing officers is fairly limited. When we have to turn on the screws we can, but it can store up problems in the future. Staff can be deliberately unco-operative, without making it obvious. The dual threats of the press and the ombudsman waved at the Director of Housing, particularly when they have been bruised and battered from a recent housing case, can be a very effective weapon. But it really is a last choice, unless the council have been particularly obstinate without good reason. This arsenal was one I kept in reserve, and thankfully didn't need to use in this case.

I arranged a meeting with the Housing Allocations Officer of the Council and took Gladys along with me. I had also asked for the presence of a member of the Council's legal team, since any decision by the Council was liable to made on legal grounds.

I have no doubt that being a Housing Allocations Officer is a tough task. You are always having to turn away quite worthy cases because you simply don't have places available. The result is that the staff themselves can come across as being hard and heartless, which they probably aren't.

A four-way discussion followed. The key decision was whether Gladys Gear had intentionally made herself homeless, as the housing officer stated, thereby forfeiting her right to be housed. We were arguing that Gladys was becoming homeless through no fault of her own.

The lawyer, as lawyers are prone to do, sat on the fence. Since this argument was the weak area in the council line, this was where we needed to apply pressure.

I asked the decisive questions.

"Did Gladys ever own the house that she lived in?"

"In a strictly legal sense, no."

"Without going to the courts, was there any way that she could continue to live in her existing house?"

"Probably not."

At this point the housing officer intervened.

"If the matter had gone to court, in your opinion, would Mrs Gear's appeal to change the terms of the will have succeeded?"

"Almost certainly."

"Almost certainly. Not absolutely certainly?" I queried.

"There was always a very slight chance that the courts would have rejected the appeal, but it is highly unlikely."

"But not impossible?"

"No."

"Had Gladys won the money, as was her husband's intention, could she have remained in her present house?"

"Of course."

"You are absolutely certain?"

"Yes. The house would have belonged to her."

We had clinched the argument and won. There was no absolute cast-iron guarantee that Gladys could have successfully challenged the will, even had she wished to. The Housing Allocations Officer promised to find Gladys somewhere to live. We left relieved at the outcome.

Gladys had lived in Oakleigh for some 50 years, and was obviously very keen to stay in the village. Despite my best efforts to find somewhere here, there was simply no place available. As she was classified as in need of emergency housing, it looked very likely that she might be housed in a semi-derelect 1960s tower block, in a particularly nasty part of Grimchester. Sleepyvale District Council and Grimchester Borough Council had set up as a joint emergency project there, but it remained their last choice option, as it was ours.

Then there was a stroke of luck, at least for Gladys. A lady had died suddenly at the Larches Sheltered Housing Flats in the nearby village of Standfast-in-Hollow. A bit of pleading and arm twisting on my part, to support Gladys, had the desired effect. Shortly afterwards, she left her long-standing dilapidated cottage for a smart, almost new, self-contained unit, with an on-site warden for the residents.

I popped in to see Gladys a few days after she moved in. She was very pleased with her new place. It was not much smaller than her old cottage. The draughts and neglect of her previous abode had been replaced by the warmth of central heating and brightly painted walls. Instead of clean and shabby, it was now clean and new. I left very happy to have played a small part in helping one of my constituents.

A few weeks went by, and then out of the blue, Gladys telephoned.

"Hello, Councillor Edwards. It's Mrs Gear. I just wanted to thank you for all of your help. I thought that I ought to tell you that I have now decided to go and live with my sister, in Australia. She's also a widow. Her husband Bernie died two years ago. She's invited me to go and stay there. She said that it's very nice there. Nice and warm. I don't really fancy another winter over here. It's so dreary. Anyway thank you for all of your help."

Then she was gone. I suppose one could have thought that all of my time had been wasted, yet there is something deeply satisfying about helping someone in trouble. I regretted nothing.

CHAPTER THIRTEEN

BE CAREFUL WHAT YOU SAY

Returning home from work one evening, I was greeted by a very excited Guinevere.

"Daddy, daddy, I got condemned for my ballet."

"Pardon?" I queried in disbelief.

"In my grade one ballet exam, I got condemned."

"Oh, I'm sorry," I sympathised, more than ever convinced that the money we were paying every week to Miss Hardwicke had been wasted.

"No, silly," she continued, "I got condemned, and my best friend Paula got highly condemned."

I would have continued to be confused had Penny not interjected. "No, Gwinny, you've got the word wrong. You were commended. Condemned means something completely different. Condemned means that you were criticised for something that you did wrong."

I now felt able to congratulate my daughter on passing her exam.

"Well done, Gwinny. Please be more careful what you say next time. Then everybody will understand what you mean."

She went off happily, singing her own little song:

"I got commended,
I got commended."

A couple of days later, I was interviewed by Dave Cumber of the Sleepyvale Clarion, about some new proposals that I had put before the Council. The conversation went something like this:

DC

Thanks for taking the time to see us.

JE

You're very welcome. Thank you for showing an interest.

DC

I understand that you've come up with some ideas to enable the public to be more aware about local planning applications. Would you like to explain your ideas?

JE

Well it's fairly simple really. At the moment it can be very difficult for ordinary people to find out what's going on locally – in planning terms. I want to make that much easier.

DC

And just how do you propose doing that?

JE

Firstly, by having displays of planning applications on every council noticeboard throughout Sleepyvale, whether the board belongs to the county, district or parish.

DC

Surely that is generally happening already?

JE

Not really. Planning applications tend to get posted up somewhere easy – sometimes it's just a lamp-post in the area.

DC

Isn't that enough? Surely that will make the people living there aware of the planning application.

JE

I don't think so. We really need to put up the lists somewhere where everybody knows they will be. And where they can easily see them. For example, there should be a planning board at the library in Mudiford, plus any other suitable public buildings.

DC

Is that it?

JE

Oh no, that's just to make people more aware about planning applications going through in their locality. The difficulty at the moment is giving people the opportunity to see copies of the actual plans themselves.

DC

And how do you propose doing that?

JE

At the moment all of the plans are held by the planning department in the council offices at Mudiford. This makes it very difficult for residents to get to. If you're working, for example, it can be very difficult to take time off of work just to go and see some plans.

DC

So how do you propose to help?

JE

Copies of all of the plans would be held by more accessible people and institutions. There would be one copy held at Mudiford Library, and one held by a nominated person or organisation in each town or village to which the application applied.

DC

I see. So who would these nominated people and organisations be? And who would nominate them? The Council?

JE

That would vary from place to place. For example, in Mudiford, it could be in the council offices themselves, but with one particular officer in the planning department specifically designated to deal with general enquiries to see the plans.

DC

And outside of the Council Offices? In other towns and villages?

JE

Ideally, elsewhere it would be either the clerk or chairman of the Parish Council. If they choose not to do it, then it could be the local district councillor.

DC

I see. But if it's so higgerdly piggeredly how is the man or woman in the street going to know who to contact?

JE

Oh that's easy. At the bottom of each planning notice would be the name and address of whoever held the plans locally.

DC

Isn't it likely that most of the plans would be kept in private houses?

JE

A lot of them. Yes.

DC

And do you actually think that councillors and suchlike would want people knocking on their door day and night to see plans that should really be viewed in the council offices?

JE

Why not? As long as they phone and make an appointment beforehand. Since most of those holding plans would be working during the day, they would be mostly available evenings and weekends, the same times that the majority of people would probably want to look at the plans.

DC

This sounds like a lot of work. Usually when I try to speak to other councillors, they claim they're too busy to even talk to me. Except at election time, of course. Then they're queuing up to give me details of their latest successes. Are you sure that they will be willing to co-operate?

JE

I hope so. Certainly those that I've spoken to have been very positive about the idea.

DC

And they didn't need any persuasion?

JE

Well, to be honest, I did suggest that it would help to raise their profile locally. I suppose that some of them could have been influenced by an ulterior motive. If they were better known locally, then obviously this might help them to be re-elected come election time.

DC

Ah! So this is really a long-term plan to get yourself elected again?

JE

Oh no. Not at all. I don't even know if I will stand again, and anyway the election is a long way off. But it is a useful leverage to get any of the more reluctant councillors on board.

DC

Ah! Earlier you said that mostly they had been positive about the idea. Now you're saying that you had to apply leverage. That sounds as if they're unenthusiastic at best.

JE

Oh no. Not at all. But if they're going to take on additional work, it's helpful to point out any benefits to them. Of course my main aim is to benefit ordinary residents.

DC

OK, so we've sorted out who will hold the copy plans, although I'm still not convinced that other councillors will share your commitment. What about the cost? Surely it will cost the council, or should I say the taxpayer, quite a lot of money. After all, there will be an awful lot of plans to duplicate.

JE

Yes there will. We probably get a couple of dozen or more planning applications every week. And I would like to see all revised plans distributed in the same way as originals. The biggest cost – copying the plans – would have to be borne by the developers. They would be required to submit an extra plan for every planning application.

DC

So you're going to stitch up the poor developers to pay for it all?

JE

I don't know any poor developers. And anyway, apart from an extra copy of the plans, the Council will meet any other costs.

DC

Ah! So the taxpayer is going to have to dig deeply in his pockets as well?

JE

Not deeply. Any costs are minimal. They are certainly outweighed by the benefits, and greater access and input from the general public can surely only make for better decisions in the council chamber.

DC

But at a price. On everyone's rates.

JE

The only costs are a few extra lists to be posted. They and the plans will be distributed by the Council's existing despatch network. There'll be a few extra drops. That's all.

DC

So you are going to load costs on all of the developers who will then pass them on to the unfortunate housebuyer.

JE

I really don't think that the cost will be very much at all. After all it's only the cost of one or two extra copies to the applicant. It would only be an excessive cost if one party, in other words the Council, paid for the whole lot.

DC

OK, well thanks for explaining it. So is that the total of your proposals?

JE

Initially, yes. My long-term goal is to allow objectors to speak at planning meetings. Come to that, let developers speak too. They could explain their proposals. Councillors could even ask them questions.

DC

How would that help?

JE

You know that at present councillors can make all sorts of amendments to planning applications by laying down conditions when an application is approved. Some of these may be totally impractical. If the applicant was there, he could tell us. Or he could suggest alternatives that would achieve what we, or the objectors, wanted

DC

You seem to have slipped your emphasis. You said that you wanted to give objectors the chance to have their say. Now you're concentrating on helping the developers.

JE

I'm keen to try and resolve objections in a constructive way. Of course, I am particularly keen that objectors to planning applications get the fullest possible opportunity to speak directly to the planning committee. It's far more effective than merely listing a summary of their objections in an appendix.

DC

That sounds like a departure from current practice:

Councillors being omnipotent. Is this part of your current scheme, and does it enjoy support among other councillors?

JE

Not yet. This is my long-term strategy. I will obviously have to be persuasive to get other councillors on board. Initially I just want ordinary residents to find out more easily what's going on in their locality. Too often they only find out about planning applications after they have been approved, and when the builders move onto the site. By then it's too late.

Dave Cumber's somewhat abrupt tone became totally different as he ended the interview. He became positively friendly, and his voice softened.

DC

Well, thank you very much for allowing us an interview. Not all of your colleagues are so obliging.

JE

Yes, I have heard that some of the councillors try to avoid doing interviews with you. I don't know why. After all, it's the easiest way to get one's ideas across to the public.

DC

One would have thought so. It's pretty tough being a political reporter on the local rag. Of course I'm looking forward to the poll tax debate when it comes up, but in the meantime, I have to find local interest stories. Otherwise my boss will start wondering whether he really needs me. Personally, I think that your ideas are terrific, and I very much hope that they all come off.

JE

Well thank you very much.

DC

So how have you been finding it John – as a new councillor?

JE

Not as difficult as I thought it would be, although I'm still amazed at how often some councillors lack any common sense.

DC (laughing)

Oh, I know. I've been doing this long enough now to have seen that. And I won't ask you to name anyone. We both know who they are. So politics aside, how's your wife putting up with all of the meetings?

JE

She's been very good about it considering how often I'm now out in the evenings. I don't think that either of us had a clue as to just how much work is involved.

DC

So are you going to buy her something special for Christmas to make up for it?

JE

Probably.

DC

Any ideas yet?

JE

Well, we're now going to a lot of charity functions and suchlike: where the people all dress up pretty smartly. Penny's got a few suitable cocktail dresses, but she'd love a fur coat for the winter, to go to them.

DC

Real fur?

JE

I don't know whether I could afford one. It would probably have to be synthetic.

DC

But money aside, you would prefer real fur?

JE

I think so. I'm sure that Penny would prefer real fur.

DC

Quite right too: anything to please the little lady. You should pop into Luxe Furs in Church Street, Grimchester. They're very reasonable. Ask for Charlie, and tell him that you're a friend of mine. That way, he'll give you a good deal. I'm sure that they'd also do HP, so you've got no excuse now.

JE

Thanks, I'll look them up.

DC

Anyway thank you, once again, for taking the time to speak to us. And good luck with the plans.

Mike Drinkwater had warned me to watch out for the press, but I have to say that the interview went really well. Dave Cumber had been positive and helpful. All right, so a few of the questions about my planning changes may have been a bit tough, but that wasn't a bad thing. After all, the councillors themselves would be looking very closely at the ideas.

A few days later, the Clarion was due to come out. Unfortunately I was a bit late that morning, so didn't have time to stop and buy a newspaper on the way to work. However, I knew that Penny would get one for me anyway.

At about eleven o' clock in the morning, I was a little surprised when Penny telephoned me at work, something she usually did only in an emergency.

"John," she said very abruptly, "I wish that you wouldn't talk to the newspapers about our private life."

With that she hung up.

Not having a clue what she was talking about, I telephoned her back. I tried to explain to her that I didn't know what she was talking about, and assured her that the interview had been about my proposed amendments to planning protocols. Penny remained unconvinced. She told me that my interview with a reporter had made the front page of the newspaper, and that I had better see for myself what they'd reported. She categorically refused to disclose anything else.

The reader can imagine the torments endured during the day, and the trepidation as I went into the newsagents on the way home to purchase a copy of the Clarion.

And there it was – a large photograph of me alongside the eye-catching headline, followed by the damning article.

"MISERLY COUNCILLOR
DEFIES THE CLARION'S ANTI-FUR CAMPAIGN

John Edwards, Oakleigh Ward Councillor on Sleepyvale District Council has completely ignored the *Clarion*'s campaign to stop the slaughter of innocent animals for the cruel greed of the despicable fur traders.

The councillor's wife was pilloried by the press.

He told your *Clarion* reporter that he was looking to buy a real-fur coat for his wife, and hoped to buy one as cheaply as possible.

Not only is he pandering to the vanity of his wife, who obviously cares nothing about the murder of wildlife for her gratification, but the skinflint Councillor thinks so little of her, that he is even trying to do it on the cheap: bargain hunting for the cheapest coat he can find.

This scandalous decision comes despite last year's poll of *Clarion* readers in which 83 percent of you said that killing animals simply to provide fur was immoral.

One again or local Councillors have shown how out of touch they are with the sensitivities of the people that they are supposed to be representing."

It took quite some persuading before Penny grudgingly accepted my explanation of how the headline could have arisen. Nevertheless, she remained in a bad mood all evening. When things had settled down slightly, I scoured the rest of the newspaper for any information on the proposed planning improvements that I was promoting. On the first read through, I couldn't find anything. A second scouring of the newspaper eventually turned up a two paragraph article at the foot of page 27.

"COUNCIL PLANS CRITICISED"

Sleepyvale District Council is to debate whether to order additional copies of plans to be made more accessible to the public.

A spokesperson for the National House Builders Federation, whose members would have to pay for the scheme, declared: 'It is very unfair asking us to bear the costs, just because the Council wants to change the way it works.'"

As Gwinny came to kiss me goodnight, she looked sad.

"Is mummy cwoss with you?" she asked innocently.

"It's not important darling. It's just something that I said to a man from the newspaper that was misunderstood," I explained.

"Oh, that's all right then," she replied, before adding wisely, "You just have to be more careful what you say next time."

As she skipped merrily off to bed, she sang her own

song:

"Daddy's been condemned-ed,
Daddy's been condemned-ed."

I pondered on Mike Drinkwater's advice about not talking to the press, and wondered whether I had done 'kerb-crawling' Councillor Brimshaw a disservice in assuming his guilt.

CHAPTER FOURTEEN

THIS LADY IS FOR TURNING

Of course anyone can make a mistake. It's whether one learns from the mistake that is important. Certainly the mere thought of a charging rogue reporter would now have me reaching for a shotgun. If I had one of course, which I haven't. As a bank clerk, I seem to have something of an instinctive aversion to shotguns.

However, a bolt from the blue introduced a prodigal constituent with even more of an ability to make the wrong decisions. On one of my few quiet evenings at home with the family, our domesticity was disturbed by somebody who I had never expected to hear from again. As usual the intrusion came via the telephone.

"Hello, Councillor Edwards. It's Gladys Gear here."

"Oh hello, Mrs Gear. How are you enjoying Australia? I bet that it's a bit warmer there than it is here at the moment." I wondered at the marvellous clarity of the call from thousands of miles away compared with the amount of noise and crackling that we get on some of our local calls.

"I expect it is. But I'm not in Australia anymore. I've come back. It was nice there. Certainly nice and warm. But I didn't really get on well with my sister. Really we never did. Even as children. Have they kept my flat at the Larches for me? I've booked into a local hotel at the moment. Just for a couple of nights. You know, while I get sorted out. I would like to get back to my own place as soon as possible. My furniture is still in storage. I do hope that they've kept the flat empty. So that it would all be ready for me. In case things didn't work out."

It was one of those rare occasions when I was lost for words. I had been advertising myself as 'the listening councillor'. On this occasion that's exactly what I did – listened – speechless. I then had to brace myself to give Gladys the almost inevitable bad news. She had been away for three months. As far as anyone knew she had emigrated for good. With the high demand for the kind of accommodation available at the Larches, it was highly unlikely that her retirement home had not been snapped up by some other deserving case. I advised her to get onto the Council Housing Department straight away.

Two days later, I accompanied Gladys to meet a less than happy Housing Allocations Officer at the Council offices. She grudgingly agreed that the Council should provide emergency housing. The drawback was where this was.

Che Guevara Towers was an ugly grey high-rise block in the Gasworks Division of Grimchester. I have already mentioned it as the last emergency refuge for the homeless – a jointly funded emergency housing project funded by Sleepyvale and Grimchester Councils. It was designed to cut the enormous bills that the Councils had been paying for almost equally dismal, and more expensive, private bed and breakfast accommodation.

This had certainly not been the intention when the flats had been put up in the 1960s. Then it was considered to provide attractive and imaginative homes fit to take council tenants into the twenty-first century. It had been designed by Sir Charles Rutherford, one of Britain's top architects, and was largely based on his own block of apartments in Manchester, which had won all kinds of awards and resulted in his knighthood.

Within five years Che Guevara Towers became a very undesirable address. Within ten years it was a slum. Within fifteen years it had become a war zone between rival gangs. No amount of award-winning design at its conception, nor any renovation afterwards, could disguise what it had become: a bleak haven for criminals, drug addicts, prostitutes and possibly sweet, old ladies who had upset the Council's Housing Allocations Officer.

I left Gladys alone for a while in her human-rat infested hell-hole. I didn't telephone her. She didn't telephone me. Although I don't suppose that there was a telephone within 400 yards of Che Guevara Towers that hadn't been vandalised.

This was merely putting off the inevitable. Eventually I plucked up the courage to write to her and ask how she was. Of course I had no way of knowing whether the Post Office still delivered there, or whether they regarded the block as a no-go zone.

Gladys wrote back to tell me that she was fine and that she had settled in well, although she considered that the block itself "could do with a bit of a tidy up". She invited me to pop in for tea on the following evening.

With some trepidation I decided to go. Still, if a poor defenceless old lady could survive there, then a fit, strapping councillor in the prime of life should have no fear. (All right, delete the fit, strapping, and add flabby, gutless.)

At the entrance to the flats, I had to step over excrement and discarded syringes and condoms, to reach the lift. This was smothered in multi-layered graffiti, and smelt of fear and urine. Thankfully it was working. On the seventeenth floor, I found my way to flat 173, and rang the bell. There was a slight pause, presumably for Gladys to view her visitor through the spyhole. Then she opened the door and shepherded me in.

Inside she had managed to make the place quite presentable – spick and span. The overall impression of slight tattiness was a sign of poverty rather than neglect. On the floor, a young half-caste girl of three or four was playing with her Barbie dolls. They benefited from a large white plastic mansion and a vast array of kitchen units and gadgets. Outside in the paddock a horse frolicked, whilst at the door to the house gleamed a bright red Ferrari. The whole incongruous scene, in the reality of a high-rise slum somehow gave the toys a surreal persona.

Over tea Gladys told me how she had settled in. Obviously her circumstances had improved somewhat since our first meeting. We now both had matching cup and saucer, and she fetched them from a sideboard where the rest of the matching set could be seen.

I had expected a diatribe about how awful the place was. Instead she was quite chirpy.

"I've met my neighbours," she said. "I get on very well with them. They're only a young couple. And they have a young child. I've been baby-sitting for them. Faith, say hello to Councillor Edwards."

Two eyes looked up suspiciously. Obviously she had been told not to talk to strangers, a sensible precaution given the location.

"Hello," she said in a surly manner.

"Hello Faith," I smiled back, having always found it easy to get on with children and pets. All of my grief seems to come from the adults.

She resumed brushing her doll's long golden hair, her own being short and somewhat curly.

"The man is charming" Gladys continued, "and very generous. As for little Faith, I've become like a grandmother to her. You know that I don't have any grandchildren of my own. My poor boy got killed in the war. In Korea."

160

I acknowledged that I knew her tragic tale.

"Of course," she continued. "The downstairs foyer needs a bit of a tidy-up. Well, if I'm honest, a lot of a tidy-up. I'm going to have a word with Ringo about it."

"Ringo? Who's Ringo?" I asked.

"Ringo Saint-Michael," she replied. "Faith is his daughter. He seems to be quite important. Well respected. Some sort of businessman, I think. There's always lots of people going to his door and giving him money. He's the only person around here that gets anything done. When the lifts all broke down none of us could get the Council to fix them. But Ringo did. He's a bit like an unofficial local tenants leader. "Aside from that, he's been a big help personally. I don't know whether you noticed, this is a bit of a rough area. But Ringo has told me that I'm quite safe here. He said that he'd put the word around that I was looking after his child, and that nobody should bother me. And they haven't."

I had allowed Gladys to run with her conversation, as I sat dumbfounded.

Now in any given area, most of us remain anonymous. However the name 'Ringo Saint-Michael' sent a shiver down my spine. Surely there couldn't be two local people with the same name.

Ringo Saint-Michael was the most notorious 'gangster' in West Anglia. Protection rackets, drug dealing, armed robbery, prostitution rings, he was linked with the lot. Nothing had ever been proved of course. Witnesses were 'accident-prone' or had the habit of 'disappearing' before trial.

We had just finished tea, and I was about to leave, when the Grimchester Godfather arrived. Considering his reputation, he was pretty unprepossessing. For a start he was short. Certainly under five-feet six-inches tall. He was immaculately dressed in a suit with exaggerated pin-stripes and a broad tie atop an expensive-looking ruffled silk shirt. The overall impact was of a slightly feminine garb.

The name 'Ringo' was certainly appropriate – chunky gold rings were on most fingers, and a large 'pirate' ring was attached to one ear. I had always believed him to be Afro-Caribbean, but his milky-coffee colour showed that there was obviously a great deal of white blood diluting the Negro in him.

'Mrs Grimchester Godfather' was slightly taller, emaciated, with a pasty-white complexion, and was decorated with even more rings, including through her nose, eyebrow, and goodness knows where else not on view. She gathered up and carried out her daughter. The toys remained on the floor.

No doubt about it, Ringo had his daughter's eyes. He looked at me in the same suspicious way as Faith had, until Gladys told him who I was – "the councillor who had got her the flat". Then he relaxed – very slightly.

He pulled out a large black leather wallet, packed with notes and counted three ten-pound notes into Gladys' hands. Then he nodded his head slightly to one side by way of acknowledgement, turned around and left.

After the door had closed, Gladys went into the kitchen and put the money into a biscuit barrel sitting on top of her wall unit.

"I do a lot of baby sitting," she said. "Ringo's really generous. Says that he wouldn't want anybody else looking after his little baby."

"Aren't you a bit worried keeping your money there?" I asked, knowing the reputation of Che Guevera Towers.

"Oh no," said Gladys in a matter-of-fact manner. "Ringo has told me that I am under his protection. He said that he will guarantee my safety, and that he regards me as a member of the 'family'."

She went on. "He's a good father. His daughter is

really spoilt. Look at all of these toys. He's only given them to her this week. It's not even her birthday."

I looked down with amazement at the vast array of 'Barbie' dolls in different costumes and all of the luxuries with which they were surrounded. I now saw Ringo Saint-Michael in an entirely different light.

I came away much surprised by the interview. Not only had Gladys Gear survived her incarceration in one of the toughest environments in the county, she was actually thriving. She had a new purpose in life, a new glint in her eye and some new money in her purse. Additionally the in-famous Ringo Saint-Michael had been shown as some-thing other than just another ruthless gangster.

Thinking about how wrong you could be about people who you had never met, I stopped on the way home to buy the latest copy of the Clarion newspaper. On the front page was an article about a ram-raiding at the Grimchester branch of Toys 'R' Us. The article made the event sound like something out of an American action movie.

Window shopping took on a whole new meaning.

A stolen Land Rover had been driven straight into the shop's plate glass window in the early hours on Sunday morning. The 'World of Barbie' display module, the central feature there, had been removed in its entirety, together

164

with a large quantity of other games and toys from inside the store. The gang had got clean away and the Land Rover had been abandoned and set ablaze in the Gasworks area of Grimchester. The report concluded with an appeal for help from the police, together with an artist's impression and a photo-fit picture of the driver and apparent gang leader, compiled from some eye-witnesses who happened to be in the area at the time.

There was something vaguely familiar about this sketch showing an apparent half-caste of mixed Anglo-Saxon and Caribbean parentage.

Was it the viciousness that the artist had somehow captured in the gang leader's eyes? I think not.

What about the cruel twisted mouth? Again no.

Perhaps it was something about the suspicious stare, loaded with distrust.

Or maybe, just maybe, it was the single large pirate earring dangling from one of the ear lobes.

CHAPTER FIFTEEN

THE CRIMINAL COUNCILLOR

One of the outside bodies, whose committee I sat on as a council representative, was the grandly named Sleepyvale Community Crime and Order Forum. This was a well-meaning consultative body with no real powers. Even its sphere of influence was a very grey area, since the West Anglian Divisional Police Authority more or less ignored any of its recommendations.

The forum met three or four times a year, usually in some dreary, draughty school hall. Membership was, in theory, open to any members of the public, but since none of the leading authorities represented at the forum went out of their to notify the public, it remained for the most part a 'private' meeting.

There were elected representatives from Sleepyvale District Council (of which I was one), West Anglian County Council and a tiny fraction of the town and parish councils invited. One or more police officers attended under sufferance, struggling the whole meeting to appear interested in the discussion, and only coming to animated life when the forum looked like making any suggestions that would interfere with their operations.

Representatives of other invited groups: the Citizens Advice Bureau, Board of Trade, Housing Associations, Tenants Groups, Senior Citizens Groups, schools, and the like, were noticeably absent.

Of all the meetings which I attended, one stands out: a

meeting held at Lower Appleton to discuss 'crime in the rural community'. Lower Appleton had been chosen as the venue because crime levels here were among the highest in any of the villages.

We sat around tables in small groups, surrounded by the paraphernalia of overhead slide projectors, display boards and other essentials to any modern presentation. On one side of me sat an elderly gentleman who introduced himself as the chairman of the Association of Mudiford Home Watches. On the other side sat the familiar face of Councillor John Walker. Councillor Walker was something of a rarity. Whilst most of the councillors were moving inexorably towards the acquisition of Zimmer frames, John drove a bright red TVR sports car. Indeed, his arrival at council meetings was heralded by the loud noise of his over-revved engine.

Instead of a delicious throaty purr from the car, he produced a raucous snarl. It was whispered among other councillors that this effect had been obtained by drilling holes in the exhaust pipes. It certainly made an impact, as if to say: "Look it's me! I've arrived! And I'm very important! I'm a councillor!"

The aim of the meeting was to reassure local residents. The theme was to be that 'the fear of crime is greater than crime itself'. The chairman welcomed us and proceeded to outline the planned agenda for the evening before introducing the first speaker.

Had Enid Blyton sought her inspiration for the character of PC Plod, it must have been someone like Constable Pender, Rural Crime Prevention Co-ordinator for Sleepyvale. For those of you whose idea of a crimefighter is 'Starsky and Hutch' or Bruce 'Die Hard' Willis, the amiable, rotund figure of PC Pender in his crumpled uniform was an anti-climax. One was left with the distinct impression that opening a jar of pickled onions would be stretching his fitness to the limit.

However, with the help of slides, he gave us the crime statistics for the past quarter. This was broken down into various categories: murder, assaults, burglary, car crime, etc. The total figure ran into thousands and made me realise just what a lawless society we had become. Constable Pender continued with arrest statistics, and finally conviction rates.

Having troubled us, he then tried to reassure us. He pointed out that compared to neighbouring Grimchester, the overall level of crime in Sleepyvale was low. It didn't look very low, but the reason for this strategy became more obvious at question time.

When asked about poor police response times, and failure even to answer the telephone at the Police Headquarters in Mudiford, we were met with the same patronising excuses: the demands on police time of crime-ridden Grimchester, and the complexity of all of the paperwork in even the simplest arrest. The overall impression given was that it was too much trouble to bother with our district except for the gravest of crimes.

One area that seemed to be giving most concern to those few local residents who had accidentally stumbled upon the meeting was juvenile crime. There was particular concern about problems at Tithebury Comprehensive where the village children went at the age of eleven. Constable Pender assured us that the problems there were no different to those of a generation earlier. He read out aloud the concluding statement of a report published in 1951, the year after the school was opened. It detailed widespread concerns about problems at the school. In particular, the general lack of respect for authority, poor discipline and the dangers of pupil behaviour causing problems in the community at large.

The idea of the presentation was to reassure the older

members of the community present, who had either attended the school themselves or sent their children there. In 1951, their greater familiarity with the school meant they would have been far more aware that everything wasn't as black as it was painted. I don't know if many of the residents were that convinced by this mental therapeutic massage, but it suited PC Pender's message that 'the fear of crime is worse than crime itself'.

We then passed on to discuss traffic problems and in particular speeding. This was to be a perennial thorn in the forum's side. At every meeting the worthy citizens complained about speeding where they lived. They then got into cars themselves, rammed down their throttles and sped off into the night, with little or no regard for any little white roundels that they might see en route. You know the ones I mean; they've got black numbers written on them, are surrounded by red circles, and are there to advise motorists of the maximum permitted speed.

This particular meeting was enlivened by the fresh air that was Councillor Walker. He had been caught speeding by the police on the way to the meeting, and put two points forcefully to the police representative.

Firstly, why were the police using mobile hand-held speeding guns to trap unsuspecting motorists, when there were so many permanent cameras already in place. He considered it very unfair that the police could step out of the shadows and stop drivers without any warning. Surely they should put up signs saying something like "mobile police speed trap ahead" to warn people, so that they could slow down beforehand. Councillor Walker's argument was that failing to do this was resulting in more motorists being prosecuted, and consequently pushing up crime figures. Were the police acting as agent provocateurs in successfully detecting speeding drivers? After all, had they not been there, nobody would have realised that the law was

169

being broken. Was this intended merely as a method to improve crime detection rates?

His second point hinged on road safety. The police claimed that the cameras were in place to cut accidents by reducing car speeds. However, Councillor Walker took the opposite viewpoint. Speed cameras created accidents. His argument went something like this:

"You're driving along perfectly safely. Say you're doing 60 miles per hour in a 30 limit. There's another car right behind you doing a similar speed. But you're both driving perfectly safely. Then suddenly you hit a sign showing a speed camera ahead. You break hard. The car behind you breaks hard as well and goes into the back of you. Far from reducing accidents, the speed camera has caused one. I do a lot of driving. I'm a very good driver. A very safe one. I drive a very good car. A very safe one. The TVR braking system is one of the best on any car. It's also got that extra power so that one can accelerate out of trouble. I've never had a child run in front of my car, but I've had loads of cars brake suddenly in front of me when they see one of these wretched signs for speed cameras. Don't you think that they should all be taken down, so that we can drive more safely and reduce accidents?"

The idea was certainly novel, although it didn't seem to have much support from most of the meeting. There were very few present under the age of 50, and one must presume that the spectre arose of a certain councillor in a bright red TVR mowing them down as they moved across the road at a sedate pace.

The agenda now moved on to crime prevention and how people could help prevent crime. The way that Constable Pender presented this, one could almost imagine that crime was all the fault of the victims. If they didn't have all of their doors and windows fitted with top of the range security locks, if they walked around carrying handbags on their shoulders for all to see, if they collected their pensions at the same time every week, if they parked their cars in areas where the streetlights had been smashed, if they expressed an opinion in the pub that other people could overhear... well, they were asking for trouble weren't they.

One wonders whether with the way that present attitudes are changing, one day in the not too distant future, victims might be arrested by the police, or sued by the criminals, for provoking crimes carried out against them.

The rationale of this argument was certainly not backed up by the figures. In Grimchester, where one may imagine that people were the most wary of crime, and therefore the most careful, crime levels were absolutely dreadful. In some of the smaller hamlets, where one may imagine residents still left their front doors unlocked, crime was exceptionally low.

Perhaps the point that the police were trying to get across is that if you're mugged, burgled, beaten up, raped or murdered, it's highly unlikely that the police will ever arrest anyone for it. If they do, then the Crime Prosecution Service are liable to throw out the case before it comes to court, and if it does get to court some clever defence lawyer has a realistic chance of getting the perpetrators off the hook. In other words, look out for yourself. It may be costing you a great deal in taxes to pay for the police, but don't rely on them to help you.

We then moved on to a general question and answer session, where members of the public who wanted to attend the meeting, and elected representatives who had been summoned to the meeting, could ask the trickiest of questions to PC Pender and his cronies on the top table.

It was here that the worthy policeman came into his own, rather than in his crime-fighting skills. His ability to fend off even the most sensible of suggestions and to dismiss the most well reasoned of arguments, was a superb show of craftsmanship. No question from however a seasoned participant troubled him. One could do nothing but admire the way either he rapidly responded to the impracticality of any suggestions, or if his ability to make such a precision response failed, he oh so skilfully failed to answer the question altogether.

Throughout this he somehow tried to convince his audience of the first rule of the local police force: the fear of crime is greater than the crime itself. He had just uttered one of his umpteen variations on this theme, when the door to the school hall was dramatically flung open, and a more mature gentleman burst in, his grey hair dishevelled by the wind.

"Ere," he said loudly. "As someone 'ere left a police car outside?"

"I have one in the car park," responded Constable Pender.

"Well you ain't no more," said our newly arrived visitor. "Some of them yobbos from Tithebury Comprehensive have just nicked it. I expect they'll drive it up to the top of Elm Hill and set fire to it, same as usual."

" Allo' Allo' Allo.
Who's set fire to my patrol car?"

Pandemonium broke out in the school hall, and the meeting came to an abrupt halt. PC Pender, and a member of the local Police Authority who had sat silently next to him throughout, left the building rapidly, presumably in the vain hope that they could avoid a police car being torched, and thereby undermining all of the platitudes given out earlier in the evening.

Some of the older residents in attendance conversed together in whispers: "We told them what it was like with the vandals around here"; "they never listen to us"; "I always knew that the crime wasn't just in our minds", etc.

As I was sitting near to PC Pender's table, and nobody else had done so, I thought it would be prudent to gather up his papers. After all, some of them might be confidential. As I gathered them, one piece of paper slipped out and fell to the floor. Had it not done so I would never have read it, for it is not in my nature to pry into things that do not concern me. However, having inadvertently seen the heading, I was mesmerised into reading the page. The contents of the paper went something like this.

COMPARISON OF PROBLEMS AT TITHEBURY COMPREHENSIVE TODAY COMPARED TO THE REPORT TO GOVERNORS OF PROBLEMS IN 1951.

NB IN NO CIRCUMSTANCES SHOULD THIS INFORMATION BE VOLUNTARILY DISCLOSED TO MEMBERS OF THE PUBLIC UNLESS IT IS UNAVOIDABLE.

PRINCIPLE CONCERNS IN 1951
1. Arriving late for class
2. Running in corridors
3. Not standing up when teachers enter the room
4. Chewing gum in class
5. Not getting homework in on time

PRINCIPLE CONCERNS TODAY
1. Truancy
2. Dinner money protection rackets
3. Assaults on staff by students in the classroom
4. Students armed with knives

5. Disruptive behaviour in class
6. Drug dealing
7. Theft, particularly car crime
8. Vandalism and Arson
9. Teenage pregnancy
10. Abusive parents

I don't know whether I was ever really taken in by PC Pender's propaganda. I certainly wasn't any longer. I thought it better not to read any of the other pages before delivering the papers back to the police station. After all, I don't want to have nightmares.

CHAPTER SIXTEEN

COME BACK WAT TYLER,
YOUR COUNTRY NEEDS YOU

Councillor John Walker of red TVR fame was to crop up again as a major player in the year's biggest political event: the replacement of rates by community charge, or poll tax as it became better known.

I can't say that I went into the controversy with any fixed view about poll tax. The idea of everybody paying something towards local council services seemed eminently sensible, and the idea of some poor old lady living by herself on a meagre pension paying more than a family of working adults seemed somewhat unfair. In either case, I wouldn't be particularly affected by the change in my own pocket, there being little difference in what Penny and I would pay in poll tax compared to what we paid in rates. Nor, for that matter, would the vast majority of people be affected.

However, this lack of any difference did not stop Poll Tax becoming the hottest political show in town. The trouble locally didn't start in Sleepyvale but in our urban neighbour Grimchester. When they came to discuss the community charge, the militant wing of the Anarchist Liberation Front occupied the council chamber, set fire to a Union Jack and inadvertently nearly burned down the town hall itself. (At least I hope it was inadvertently.)

With the community charge debate about to descend upon Mudiford, councillors of all political persuasions began to flex their oratory muscles.

The Councillors' Martial Arts Group.

Councillor John Walker went one step further. He was apparently a brown-belt in one of those obscure martial arts groups, which pop up periodically and then disappear without trace, or more probably reappear under a new name.

Councillor Walker made it clear that he relished the coming confrontation with the forces of 'Law and Disorder', having convinced himself, if not many others, that he would, personally, physically expel any anarchists, socialists, communists or whatever, who dared to disrupt the council meeting. However, he realised that he couldn't take on a mob single-handed, so tried to recruit an army of council-warriors, having arranged two evening sessions the week before for any councillors that wanted to learn unarmed combat in his chosen style.

I cannot say what response he had, as I chose not to go there myself. However, the knowledge that most of the council chamber was full of people of declining years, for some of whom simply getting out a chair and standing up was a physical challenge, I suspect any uptake was small.

For the rest of us, we relied on 'Gimpy' Jones, who combined the roles of security and pomp. His duties ranged from announcing the arrival of the chairman to, theoretically, ejecting troublesome members of the public from the public gallery. As 'Gimpy' was of an advanced age, and had lost a leg in the evacuation of Dunkirk, it was fortunate that he was able to use his limited charm as a weapon to achieve his security duties. One certainly could not see him forcibly ejecting a mob of anarchists, even with the help of Councillor Walker and his merry band.

The debate began with a motion from one of the Labour Councillors condemning the introduction of the "iniquitous poll tax", and calling upon the Council to refuse to set a community charge in protest. One can perhaps forgive his willingness to break the law in his opposition to something that he passionately hated. However, his attempt to introduce this in a council where the overwhelming majority of councillors were Conservatives who fully supported the government changes, can only be regarded as so stupid as to be farcical.

Not, of course, that there was to be any rational attempt to discuss the issue. Everyone was far too busy getting on their high horses to worry about anything remotely infected with logic. Indeed, the Labour councillor who had started thing was acting as no more than a referee's whistle, and now that the game was started every one queued up to have a pop at one side or the other.

The most incredible of the speeches actually came from the Conservative benches. One came from an extremely decrepit looking individual of advanced years, whom I had never seen speak before, nor would ever see speak again. However, once started his imbecilic rambling went on without end.

"I think," he started in a slow ponderous manner, as if tasting every sentence in his mouth before spitting it out. "I think that the Pole tax is a good thing. After all we did for them in the war, it's about time that we taxed them. After all we did for them, tck, tck, to go and invite the Russky Commies in. What ingratitude."

One or two of those fellow Conservatives sitting near him were sufficiently awake to realise that their illustrious colleague was going completely off the political rails and tried to reign him in, but he would have none of it.

"Don't you interrupt and shsh me, I know what I'm talking about. The Poles should pay us, and the Czechs and the Hungarians, after all we did for them. And the Greeks. Especially the Greeks. I don't like them, don't trust them."

The other councillors sat back and let him get on with it: the Conservatives with concerned looks on their faces, the rest of us with amusement.

The discussions went on. Well, perhaps that's the wrong word, as there was nothing remotely constructive about the vicious arguments that took place. Not only was the policy of the introduction of community charge put through the meat grinder but Councillors also indulged in wholesale personal abuse against one another. Perhaps nothing was more childish than the references to Scotland and the Scots.

It started when Councillor Jimmy McDonald, an exile from that northern part of the United Kingdom, pointed out the failure of the community charge in Scotland. It had been introduced there a year earlier than in the rest of the country to see how well (or not) it worked. There it had provoked widespread and persistent opposition, and 20 percent of the population had not paid a penny of it by the end of the first year.

As Jimmy said: "Poll Tax has been a total and utter failure in the Scottish trials, so why should it be inflicted upon the residents of Sleepyvale, when it has been seen to fail so miserably in one of the English colonies."

This played right into the hands of one of the hard-line *English* Tories.

"Just because community charge may have failed north of the border, and I only say may, is that any reason to dismiss it out of hand here? I say a resounding NO it's not. One only has to look at the things that the Scots like, but we don't, to see that."

He paused to take breath, before launching into a diatribe of absurdity.

"The Scots love haggis. Do we like to dine on a sheep's stomach full of porridge?" A murmur of "no" came from the benches around him.

"The Scots like to wear kilts. Do we? Of course not." Again the murmur concurred.

"The Scots idolise that Robbie Burns fellow. Call that incomprehensive twaddle poetry? Give me Wordsworth or Tennyson any time. And as for 'Our Wullie' it isn't remotely funny. By contrast, here in England we have marvellous comics. Of course I read the Eagle, but even the working class comics, like the Beano and Dandy, have some amusement value.

"I hope that my colleagues would agree with me when I say that there is little in the fields of Scottish art, literature and music that is to our taste, and I dare say that they say the same about us."

In the midst of the support for this viewpoint on the Tory benches, I recalled with affection, and without any difficulty, reading great Scottish books, *A child's garden of verse* and *Treasure Island*, and watching *Ivanhoe* on television. I have a vague recollection that Roger Moore might have played the lead before succeeding well-known Scottish actor Sean Connery in the role of James Bond. Come to think of it, weren't the Beano and Dandy printed in Dundee? Readers may judge for themselves how my mind wandered off into daydreams whilst a certain councillor switched his attention to extolling the virtues of morris dancing, the bowler hat, etc.

At last he came to the end. "And so colleagues, I have to put it to you, that all of the evidence points to the indisputable fact that where something is unsuccessful in Scotland, it invariably means that it is a resounding success here in England."

He finished to a chorus of 'Here Here'.

Inevitably the Conservative majority won the vote some hours later, when the politicians had talked themselves to a standstill. Our Council would be supporting the poll tax.

I voted with the opposition, although, unlike almost everyone else present, my reasons were not ideological. Like it or not, we're all going to clobbered for tax anyway, and like Mr Ordinary, most of us wouldn't be greatly affected one way or the other. A far wiser man than I said something to the effect that the best taxes were those that were cheap and easy to collect. If that is indeed the first tenet of a good tax, then the community charge has to be considered a total failure.

The initial budget was already in preparation for next year and we'd received a first draft proposal. Among the minor changes from the previous year was one very substantial increase: in salaries, postage, printing, stationery and support costs for that wing of the council's finance department responsible for collecting local taxation.

There were notes at the bottom of the page designed to explain such variations, and discourage councillors from popping up and down at meetings asking why such-and-such had gone up so much. In this case the point should not have been lost on those councillors who opposed the poll tax for reasons of ideology, when their efforts would have been better spent on fighting the huge additional cost of collection.

In the case of Sleepyvale, the staff costs alone were the employment of 12 permanent full-time staff to handle the increased administration, and a further eighteen full-time staff for the first year of introduction. Sleepyvale is only a very small part of the country, yet here alone it was going to cost the taxpayer over half-a-million pounds extra to collect the tax. Whatever must the cost be nation-wide for one silly woman's changes?

Finally, I can't go without a mention of Councillor John Walker's martial arts display. He warmed up with a series of threatening gestures, accompanied by a kind of high pitched squeaking, as if he'd just had a sensitive tooth bite onto an ice lolly. Behind him stood four others from the Conservative ranks of the great and the good. They all copied the actions of their leader, although even the closest of their friends could not have said that their actions had much in the way of enthusiasm or martial threat. Nevertheless Sleepyvale Dad's Army were ready and willing to throw back the hordes of lefties and tear down their red flag.

Fortunately their mettle was not put to the test. Apart from the usual reporter from the *Clarion*, the public gallery was empty. Well, it stood to reason that it would be didn't it? After all, England were playing soccer against Italy, and it was live on the television.

CHAPTER SEVENTEEN

PLANNING PROGRESS

Despite the often virulent public debate over major issues, such as poll tax, away from the bear-baiting pit of the council chamber councillors were sane, rational people, like you or me. Oh, hang on – like you, now I suppose I am one of them too.

Anyway, for several months I persevered with my plans to publicise planning applications, looking forward to a tasty dessert later, when members of the public would be officially permitted to open their mouths and speak directly to the planning committee.

It was all a matter of patience. One needs a great deal of it as a councillor. The world whizzes through space at an alarming pace, all the while wobbling, and at the same time spinning at the speed of a jet aircraft. Yet we don't notice the motion. Our concept of it comes from the change around us, not the movement: day to night, summer to winter. To anyone who had taken an interest in following my ideas to fruition, nothing seemed to be happening. Yet behind the scenes I had been working hard, whittling away at individual councillors to persuade them to support me on the idea of a wider dispersal of planning information. Those reckless enough to show even a reasonable interest were then burdened with stage two of the plan.

My finest conquest, which spurred me on greatly, was Councillor Timothy Darcy, leader of the Conservative

Party.

The ruling elite on the Council included those destined for high office, such as chairman of the council, and those key decision makers who actually ran things, such as committee chairpersons. Of course, the same person could have a foot in both camps, but certain individuals of long-standing service, but little ability, could aspire to the highest office.

Councillor Albert Hepple was Chairman of the Sleepyvale District Council because of his great patience, rather than any brilliant political mind or dynamic ideas. True he oversaw full council meetings, trying to control the unruly mob whom the electorate, in their infinite wisdom or folly, had chosen to represent them. Yet his main role was to represent the council at civic functions, charity fund-raising events and the like. He held the office because he wanted to do it, and because it was his turn among the senior Conservatives. His reward, if indeed chairman of the council can be considered a reward, was for his patience in living long enough.

Councillor Timothy Darcy was a far more important, and indeed capable, councillor. As leader of the party holding the majority, and chairman of the council policy and strategy committee, he played prime minister to Albert Hepple's constitutional monarch.

I had sought an early meeting with him, but it took some weeks before he could fit me into his busy schedule. Apart from leading us, he was a County Councillor on West Anglia County Council and a representative on the fire, police, and health authorities. Add up the total expenses claimable on all of these and he was on a nice little earner. But I digress.

I explained my ideas. He listened intently and asked sensible questions. The idea of "Himself" becoming better known by Joe Public seemed a particularly tempting carrot for him. He was quite open to the idea of more publicity, even though he didn't fancy the idea of storing plans himself for the public to view. His manner was somewhat condescending, even though he meant well. Let me demonstrate.

"So, Master Edwards," he began "exactly what is all of this fuss that you've been making about greater public awareness on planning issues?"

This was simply his manner. There was no hostile intention. Perhaps he thought of himself as a kind of father figure to one of the new boys on the block (well in the chamber actually), or maybe a paternal grandfather thinking back to younger, keener days.

Timothy was sharp, intelligent, and at times ruthless, behind his benign façade. He was to prove a particularly useful ally, both at this time, and with later half-conceived ideas that I gave to him. He had that ability to look at the seed of an idea and know how to bring it to full flower. If he liked to take the full credit for the idea in the first place, one can hardly begrudge him that.

Having listened, he was positive but non-committal. He said that he would discuss the ideas with the chief planning officer before coming to a decision. In the meantime, he suggested that I see the chairman of the planning committee to try to get her on board.

The Chair of Planning was less enthusiastic. Councillor Mrs Ann Hillyard added the post to that of being Council Vice-Chair. She was an amiable enough woman but she was a very timid speaker: we all strained to hear everything she said at meetings. She was actually quite competent and very knowledgeable about planning issues, but innately shy. I came away with the impression that she wasn't against the ideas, but simply couldn't face trying to explain them all to the committee and answer questions. The thought of having later to fend off members of the public doubtless filled her with dread.

A couple of weeks later, Timothy Darcy reported back that the planning officers were against the idea, but had been very vague about why – "lots of extra work for us" and that kind of thing. In the circumstances, Timothy said that he would support the plans for a trial period, with a review at the end of six months to decide whether they should continue. He was even prepared at a later date to consider the idea of allowing members of the public to speak, but not straight away. "We don't want to be rushing into anything we might regret later, Master Edwards, do we?"

What was even better than his personal support was the effort to tell his fellow Conservatives that he supported the plan, and to propose that party members have a free vote on the issue when it came to council. Without the support of at least one leading Conservative, my aspirations were doomed to failure. With Councillor Darcy's support, I now felt free to approach other members of his party who served on the planning committee.

Elsewhere I had a mixed response from Conservative members of the committee: one or two interested, one or two totally opposed and the remainder indifferent. However, one quirk of councillor behaviour that I had noticed during my period as a councillor, had begun to worry me.

On a number of occasions I have sat on committees and seen individual councillors lavish with their praise and support for something, and then vote against the same thing at a later meeting.

**Even with his parrot in support
Councillor Drinkwater was of little use**

This was most perplexing. It meant that even if the planning committee approved the idea, those same councillors might not support it at subsequent meetings, or at the full council meeting where it would finally need to go for approval.

As an example, I had seen one councillor at a meeting

of the leisure committee, eloquently outlining the case for providing a crèche at Mudiford Sports Centre to enable young mothers to take advantage of the facilities so woefully under-used during the day. Yet at the meeting of council policy and strategy committee which would have to approve its incorporation as a 'growth' item (one requiring additional expenditure in the following year's budget), the same councillor opposed it. He put forward a very powerful case that although the scheme would be very useful, there were far more important areas that merited additional funding by the Council.

Whatever support I gathered for my ideas could, therefore, not be guaranteed to be carried forward from one committee to the next. You don't have to have a split personality to be a councillor, but on the other hand it doesn't seem to do you any harm.

Mike Drinkwater had already agreed to support my plans at the full council meeting, but that was no use to me on the planning committee where he couldn't vote. Indeed, he even had to get advance approval from the committee chair before being allowed to speak, and then only on matters that concerned his own area.

I was the only member of the Campaign for Rural Advancement and Protection to sit on the planning committee. One of my key aims, therefore, had to be talking to as many other councillors on the committee as possible to sell them my proposals before they appeared on any agenda.

Although it would be possible to sway some of them with a passionate speech on the night, many would have already made up their minds in advance, either by reading the council officers' preamble or from discussions with other members of the council.

Councillors from the smaller parties (Labour, Liberals, Social Democrats, Greens, etc.) were mostly flattered at being approached. The very concept of trying to move things forward in a constructive, non-party political way seemed somewhat novel to them. (It's amazing what one can achieve through procedural ignorance and naivety.) They seemed far more comfortable in just criticising plans brought to the Council with the apparent support of the ruling Conservatives, than they were in helping to build a cross-party consensus.

Eventually Councillor Darcy reported back.

"Bad news I'm afraid, Master Edwards. Not only do officers not like it, but they have calculated that it will cost £28,000 in a full year to implement stage one, and a further £86,000 a year to allow 'your' members of public to speak."

I found the figure staggering, and queried why it was so high. Timothy then read me a list of items, from the purchase of an overhead projector to upgrading the council's public address system, together with hundreds of hours of extra officer time. They were even pushing for an extra member of staff just to deal with the mechanics of public participation. Hardly any of the listed items seemed really necessary to implement my plans.

Were they trying to sabotage the idea, or were they simply using it as a convenient hook on which to hang purchases and changes that they wanted to make anyway? In later years, I was to realise it was yes on both counts. However despite all these obstacles, Councillor Darcy, said he would still support the introduction of the scheme for a trial period.

"Of course, we'll have to knock off most of the items on the Chief Planning Officer's wish list. I'm sure that you'll agree with me, Master Edwards, when I say that most of this shopping list is unwarranted in this grand scheme of 'ours'."

"Of course," he added, "even if the planning committee approve it, it will still have to go to the Council policy and strategy committee, since only they can authorise the additional expenditure. Still, we'll see what we can do."

Having such a high powered councillor on board was certainly going to be a great asset.

So the outlook still looked hopeful – I would just have to jump through more hoops to reach my goal. It probably shouldn't be called *my* goal any more. Timothy Darcy had called it *our* scheme. As time passed he began to take over full personal ownership of the idea. Only a few weeks later he was able to telephone and leave a message on my answer-phone which went something like this:

"Hello, Master Edwards. Councillor Timothy Darcy here. My scheme to better inform the public on planning matters will be discussed at the next meeting of the planning committee. As you showed such keen interest in my idea, I wanted you to be among the first to know."

It's a good job that that I hadn't come up with the plans just to massage my own ego.

CHAPTER EIGHTEEN

TO STRIP OR NOT TO STRIP,
THAT IS THE QUESTION

It was towards the end of my first year as a councillor when I had the most unusual encounter so far with the eccentricity of ordinary folk. A voice, which I had never expected to hear again, came out of the blue.

"MISTER Edwards! Mrs Parslip here!" (Somehow she had still not been able to accept my election.) "When are you going to do something about this dreadful pollution in the village?"

This was an ideal chance to build bridges with my most implacable foe in Oakleigh. I was keen to do so and consequently even more attentive than usual.

"Hello, Mrs Parslip. Are you well?"

"The state of my health is NOT your concern. What is your concern is protecting me and the rest of the village from this appalling pollution."

"I'll do whatever I can," I offered. "Exactly what kind of pollution are we talking about?"

"The airwaves, MISTER Edwards, the airwaves."

"Do you mean from cars?" I asked, trying to be helpful.

"No, of course not! They're a necessary evil. No, it's this dreadful filth that some of the TV channels are polluting the atmosphere with. Is it right that I have to pay a TV licence only to be bombarded with pornography? We're literally choking with the obscenity. Now, how are you going to bring clean air back to the village."

This was not going to be easy.

"Well I'm sorry, Mrs Parslip, but I really don't have any say in what television programmes are shown. It tends to be the commercial channels that are challenging some of the existing boundaries of what is considered acceptable to veiwers – Channel Four in particular. But you don't pay for them. It's only the BBC. that receives revenue from television licences"

Mrs Parslip was becoming more agitated.

"Lot of filth on their channels too. So, even though you're our local councillor, you can't bc bothered to protect the village from pornography like that dreadful 'Truth or Bare' programme."

"I'm very sorry, but I simply don't have any influence over television programmes. I couldn't stop it, even if I wanted to."

The last comment sort of slipped out, and I knew immediately I said it that it was the wrong thing to say.

"Well, I'm not surprised. You councillors are all alike. You're always saying that you're going to do things but when it comes down to it, you never do what we want. It sounds to me like you support this filth. I'm sure that if you really wanted to you could stop these obscenities being broadcast. Still, I'm not surprised. I've dealt with you long enough to know that you're pathologically incapable of doing things properly."

And with her passing darts, Mrs Parslip was gone, and destined to remain an implacable foe.

After the relief of putting the telephone down, I pondered on what Mrs Parslip had said about the new quiz show 'Truth or Bare'. I pondered on it – with relish. She was right about me not wishing to stop it, not that I could have any way.

You see, now that I am a councillor, I don't get many

quiet evenings at home when I can sit and watch television. As a result, I had missed the first episode. However, it had been front page news in the tabloid newspapers. The response at the bank where I worked was even more marked. Absolutely everybody was talking about it, and I seemed to be the only one who hadn't seen it.

The rules of the game show were simple; so if they sound complicated as I try to explain them, then that is down to my ineptness. Each contestant was allowed seven incorrect answers. For correct answers they won cash prizes the value of which increased as the game progressed. For every incorrect answer, they had to remove an item of their clothing. Somebody off stage had presumably already ensured agreement on what the seven items of allocated clothing were.

First, the contestant would be given the category of the question. They would then decide whether to play 'Truth or Bare' or to pass. If they passed they were out of the game and simply took away the money that they had already won. Obviously in the early stages contestants would be expected to gamble on the right answer. If it meant losing their shoes for a wrong answer they would take the chance. In the later stages, they would still be tempted to gamble. They could win big cash prizes or lose as much of their dignity as they cared to chance. They still got to keep all of the money won on earlier questions.

Anyone brave enough to play to the bitter end with seven wrong answers would finish up on stage with a fistful of cash, wearing nothing but a brave smile. To encourage them to play on, they would be given three plausible answers to chose from.

Let me give you a hypothetical scenario.

QUESTIONMASTER:
The subject is football stadiums. And the question is

194

worth £100. Do you wish to play or pass?

CONTESTANT: Play.

QUESTIONMASTER: Which English League Club plays at Fish Park? Is it:

(a) Grimchester United

(b) Grimsby Town

(c) Hull City?

A correct answer won the £100. A wrong answer and the contestant would shed an item of clothing before moving on to the next round. Had they decided to pass they were eliminated.

Although with both a wrong answer or a pass they kept money won in previous rounds, the elimination if you passed was a very strong incentive to carry on playing, even if you hadn't a clue about the subject on offer.

The quiz show had an additional element with the same appeal to man's baser instincts: a modern version of the Roman arena, where spectators decided the fate of the gladiators with a thumbs up or thumbs down. Members of the audience all had mini-monitors that flashed A, B or C, to show them the correct answer. If the contestant guessed correctly an enthusiastic compere would declare it to be 'Truth' and remind them of how much money they had just won. But if it was the wrong answer then he kept quiet. Instead an even more enthusiastic audience would chant 'Bare!' and the unfortunate contestant would not only fail to win money that time, but would have to remove an item of clothing before the baying mob.

Apart from the main quiz, at one point during the show, the main studio lights would flash on and off and a Klaxon would sound. This indicated that the contestant could opt to gamble on a question for an exotic holiday (if they won) or pay a forfeit (if they lost).

So how did the first show go, and why was I so keen to see the next edition?

It was a huge success.

My male colleagues at the bank are not usually so forthright in talking among themselves about the female of the species. They're all rather stiff and polite. Yet on the day after the show, they couldn't stop talking about a gorgeous 19-year old honey blonde who had finished up stripped down to a tiny pair of white panties, which she decided not to risk on a question about 'Greek Philosophers'.

The girls were equally forthright about a young fireman on the show who had likewise opted out with just a pair of Y-fronts left to gamble with. He had just failed to win a holiday in the Maldives, and as forfeit for his failure had finished up sitting on the laps of a coach party of middle-aged matrons from the Women's Institute, whose behaviour was certainly not that usually associated with such a lofty organisation.

There were record numbers of complaints about the show, even though it was screened after the nine o'clock water-shed when such programmes were permitted. There were general objections to the show itself, and specific disputes about whether the age limit of contestants should be 18 as the television watchdogs were insisting, rather than the 16 that the programme organisers had suggested. The programme organisers even threatened to retaliate by producing a children's version of the show, although this idea was rapidly dropped in view of the outrage that this suggestion had caused.

I couldn't really see what the fuss was all about. After all, what is so wrong with the human body that it shouldn't be shown in all its glory? Or am I just being lecherous?

Penny had been very coy when asked what she thought about the programme, from which I gathered she had found it entertaining, but I also suspect that the fireman had been sexually stimulating.

Penny and I sat down to dinner together, the children having eaten earlier. We had barely finished when the telephone rang again.

"Oakleigh 3605."

"Hello, is that Councillor Edwards?"

"Yes it is. How can I help?"

"My name is Gerald Smithcombe. I would like to see you urgently. It would only take a few minutes and I wondered if you could somehow fit me in this evening."

I looked at my watch. It was twenty past seven – still time to see him and watch my television programme.

"I could fit you in now, if it won't take too long," I offered. "I have another appointment at nine o'clock," I lied.

"Right. Thanks. I'll come round right away."

Penny had to go out for an hour, which meant that theoretically I was supposed to herd the children towards bed, but I didn't have time. Twenty minutes after the initial call, I was showing a thin sickly-looking middle aged man with a wispy beard into the lounge. If you can remember 'Catweazel' you'll have an idea of what he looked like.

He was offered tea or coffee. He opted for herbal tea and I was just about to say that I doubted whether we had any, when he produced a dainty packet with pastel coloured flowers on it, containing a solitary tea bag.

The Councillor was thinking about a naked woman when he found a naked man sitting in his lounge.

"Would you like to try one?" he offered reaching for his pocket.

"Thanks, but I'll stick to my Nescafe, I think. Please sit down and make yourself at home," I said, and went off into the kitchen to make our drinks.

I had just finished making the coffee and herbal tea

when Gwinny came into the kitchen cupping her hands over her mouth and sniggering.

I had to smile back. "What are you laughing at?" I asked.

"At that funny man in the lounge," she sniggered.

"That's not very nice is it? He can't help how he looks."

"No, it's not how he looks, silly" she replied, "it's because he's got no clothes on."

"What?" The smile left my face.

"He's got no clothes on. He's all nudey" she replied with sincerity.

Quickly I left the kitchen for the lounge. Had I inadvertently let a paedophile or pervert into my house?

Sure enough, Gerald Smithcombe was sitting naked in a comfy armchair, his clothes in a neat pile on another chair.

"Excuse me, exactly what do you think that you're doing?" I asked irritably.

"Just making myself comfortable, like you told me to" replied my guest unperturbed.

"But you've taken all of your clothes off."

"Yes," he responded in the same bland manner.

"Why?"

"Well," came the explanation, "you said to make yourself comfortable, so I have. I'm always more comfortable in my natural state; more in tune with nature and my surroundings."

I was marginally more relaxed now that I realised that my guest was some sort of eccentric naturist, although it was really only later that I was able to see the funny side.

"Well, please put something on that will make me more comfortable," I requested.

Reluctantly Gerald dressed himself and sat down. I excused myself and went off and fetched the drinks that I had made earlier from the kitchen. They were tepid now, but I didn't want to reheat them in case I received any more nasty surprises. Nor did I want to miss the beginning of my show. I was half muttering "disgusting" to myself, which was just a tiny bit hypocritical. After all, his was an innocent nakedness, unlike my own lewd desire to see some pretty young girl strip off completely on the television show 'Truth or Bare'.

Once I felt comfortable we began.

"So, Gerald, how can I help you?"

"Well, I'm branch secretary of the National Union of Disciples of Eden. It's the turn of our branch to host our national conference. As we've been having trouble finding a suitable venue we've been trying to enlist the support of local councillors."

"I see. Well, I'm afraid that I've not heard of your organisation. Do you need a large venue?" I enquired.

"Yes. We can expect at least three thousand members to attend, maybe many more."

"So, what's been the trouble finding a local venue?"

My guest elaborated: "Let me explain our organisation's beliefs and philosophy. In the beginning Man was perfect and without sin, and happily living in the Garden of Eden. He only lost that innocence in Utopia when he began wearing clothes. Instead of being worshipped as Mother Nature God's finest creation, the human body became associated with sin and depravity. We believe that to return to our natural state will help us to become a more just and civilised society. False Judaeo-Christian morality only impedes that."

"You're entitled to your beliefs of course, but why are they causing you problems in finding a venue?"

Gerald continued: "You say that we are entitled to our beliefs, yet we are not. In fact we are persecuted for them."

"Surely not," I remonstrated, "nobody is persecuted

for their beliefs nowadays."

"Well, we are," he insisted. "Sikhs can get away without wearing crash helmets because their religion says that they must wear turbans. Muslim women can wear their all-enveloping 'blankets' with their faces held behind masks. Yet if we so much as step into our gardens au naturale in accordance with our beliefs then we are promptly arrested. Yet we are keeping up a proud tradition. Did you know that Greek athletes in the Olympic Games competed for several centuries: completely naked? It was the Christians who banned the games and persecuted the athletes because of the competitors deep respect for their own bodies which they saw as a homage to the Gods.

Did you know that Celtic warriors went into battle naked to show their bravery? And that Celtic women were the equals of men, and fought alongside them. None of this legislation, like that we have now, was needed to enforce equality.

We are the descendants of those proud traditions. The racial foundation of the British people are the Celts, the foundation of British culture and civilisation comes from the Greeks. Yet we cannot carry on that tradition without being arrested and charged with offences entirely related to our beliefs.

"We are completely tolerant of other peoples beliefs. These new religions such as Christianity always want to impose their opinions on us. Most of today's conflicts in the world come from one or other of these religions trying to impose their will. We may not be in danger of being killed for our beliefs as is happening in most of the world, but we are nevertheless being persecuted."

Gerald may have had some valid points in his argument, but I still thought of him as a crank.

"I'm sorry," I replied, "but a lot of people would find your nudity offensive."

"But why? Our nudity is totally innocent. Why can't that be acceptable when a television programme like 'Truth or Bare' can be shown. There is public nudity on that. It's lewd and smutty. Why is innocence persecuted and decadence promoted?"

Without thinking, I looked at my watch to see how the time was going. Still OK.

"Anyway, Gerald, how exactly can I help?" I tried to hurry things forward.

"At your next full Council meeting, there will be application for our regional conference to be held at Mudiford Leisure Centre. I would like to think that you would be reasonable enough to support our application."

"I see. But why is this going to the Council to decide? Surely it's up to the management team at the Leisure Centre to decide. I'm sure that we would have delegated responsibility to them to sort out bookings. If the centre is free, and you are willing and able to pay the cost of hire, I cannot see why they wouldn't allow you to book."

Gerald explained: "The management would have. It was some of the local Mudiford councillors who have put a block on us. They said that they didn't want that sort of thing going on at Mudiford."

"What sort of thing?" I asked, half knowing the answer.

"Well, all disciples are expected to adhere to the strictest non-dress code whilst attending the conference."

"I see. Well that shouldn't be a problem should it? After all this is a private booking isn't it?"

Gerald continued to enlighten me: "Yes. However we do open our doors for any members of the public who wish to pop in. Other councillors have also expressed concern that, in their words not mine, we would embarrass and might corrupt the staff."

"Ah, now I begin to see where we have problems. You

entice members of the public in and force them to adopt your ways. Presumably you would also expect the staff to strip off for you."

"Of course not," he replied indignantly. "Neither members of the public nor staff are expected to adhere to our code. They need to understand our philosophy apart from anything else. We believe in the absolute and un-equivocal freedom of followers of other religions and cultures to dress as they please.

No, we invite the public in, and they are at liberty to walk around fully dressed. We expect members of staff to be fully dressed when we arrive. The problem that they all have is that they rapidly begin to feel uncomfortable being the only ones dressed when everyone else is in their natural state. Imagine if you were walking naked through a shopping centre when everyone is clothed, and you realise how out of place you would feel. So most of our visitors leave quickly, but some do join us. Some of the Mudiford councillors consider that we're corrupting their constituents."

"Well, I would have thought that their constituents could make up their own mind on that," I replied positively. "After all they are consenting adults aren't they?"

Then a thought struck me. "They are consenting adults aren't they? This is an event for the over 18s."

"Now, you see, you are making the same sexual links that I keep telling you are outside of our beliefs," he replied.

"I agree that it is up to individual constituents to make up their minds," he continued. "As to the other question: our conference is a family affair. Amongst delegates, most bring their families, so grandparents come along and children come along. Whether you are 2 or 102 you are welcome to share in the glory of Eden."

"Now I see why you're having problems," I replied.

"Yes," Gerald continued, "but the really big problem that some of you have is that passers-by can see us inside, and we also like to go outside to hand out leaflets and to explain our philosophy. Of course we inevitably attract gawping teenagers, the sort of curious 10 to 16 year-olds. But we're always happy to explain about the Disciples of Eden and to invite them to come in and look around. We also like to walk into the town centre to shop and to eat. The food in these leisure centres is usually pretty ropy."

"So you want to walk around Mudiford town centre… naked?" I asked in disbelief.

"Well, why not? After all we're perfectly happy to let you come into our conference fully clothed. You know we've been getting a bit of bad press lately. We've had a number of our disciples who have streaked at major sporting events in the last couple of years. Unfortunately the press was only interested in their perceived salaciousness rather than the message we were trying to put across."

"Really? Don't tell me that Bazooka Brenda is one of your Disciples?" I asked with fond memories of an attractive well-built girl who had streaked at three televised soccer matches this year. I kept hoping that the television channels might come to Fish Park to film Grimchester United, and that we would get the chance to see her 'in the flesh' so to speak, but so far I had been disappointed.

"Yes, she is," replied Gerald. "We're very proud of our Brenda – she comes from the militant wing of the Disciples of Eden.

"Hmm. Well you'll have to let me think about all of this," I replied, not at all certain about my own opinion, and anxious not to miss the start of the much anticipated television programme starting shortly. Give me your phone number and I'll phone you in a few days."

At this point Penny came to my rescue. Having just returned from visiting a friend. Her arrival ensured that there would be no protracted departure.

"You'll have to excuse me now I'm afraid," I muttered, shepherding my guest to the front door.

He exchanged greetings with Penny on the way out. Then he was gone.

"Who was that dear?" asked Penny.

"Some eccentric nudist who wants to bring thousands of other nudists to Mudiford for a conference."

Penny spoke without really thinking far ahead. "Hmm, sounds like a good idea. Good for tourism I should think. Fill up the hotels, help the local businesses, that sort of thing. Could help to put Sleepyvale on the map."

"Gwinny!" Penny called upstairs, "it's time you were in bed. You've got school tomorrow."

Guinevere and Arthur came down the stairs together. Gwinny started singing one of her made-up songs. This invention was called: 'I know something you don't know'.

"What's that dear?" Penny asked with interest.

"Not telling you. It's a secret."

"All right then. Off you go to bed." Penny exchanged kisses with our daughter.

Gwinny then dutifully kissed me before going upstairs. The sound of her song 'I know something you don't know' faded into the distance.

"Whatever's she talking about? Singing about?" Penny asked.

"I know," piped in Arthur quickly.

"So do I dear," I intervened. "I'll tell you about it later. Right Arthur, time you finished your homework and went to bed as well."

"Oh, do I have to? I want to stay up and watch this great new quiz show that's on the tele soon. Everyone at school watched it last week and said it was really wicked."

"Well I think perhaps I'd better watch it first to make

sure that it's suitable before you see it. I've heard a lot of bad things about it already. I'm not sure that it's the sort of thing that I would want you to watch," I replied pompously. It took a bit more leverage, but eventually Arthur went up to his room.

I thought that I must really get my video player fixed. I'm away at meetings so much that I often miss my favourite television programmes. I'm going to miss the next two episodes of 'Truth or Bare' because of council meetings. Yes, I must fix the video, then we can tape the show and watch it in peace and quiet later on.

We closed the lounge door and switched on the television. It was a bit like that guilty feeling Penny and I used to feel before we were married. You may remember the sort of thing yourself. We'd be settling down on her parents' couch late in the evening for some serious fondling, with as yet an undisclosed destination. Her parents would have just gone up to bed and as they left would tell us not to stay up too late. That wasn't meant as an invitation for Penny and me to go upstairs together, just a polite reminder to go home before things went too far on the sofa.

We switched on – just in time. Two rows of teeth, brilliant white, topped a garish royal blue sequinned jacket. It was the host Tony 'Rumpty Tumpty' Day.

"Good evening everybody. And an especial good evening to all you lecherous men and you naughty, sexy ladies. Welcome, welcome, to another edition of the nation's favourite quiz show: 'Truuuth or Baaare'. The whole audience joined in the stretched out programme name.

"Welcome, welcome once again. Who, in their right mind wants to watch 'Mastermind', when you can see instead our groundbreaking 'Dirty-mind' show?" Tony waved his arms about enthusiastically as he spoke.

He continued: "So just what has happened to last week's two lucky contestants? Have they been getting lots of public exposure? Terry, what's the lovely Lisa-Jayne been up to?"

A voice-over accompanied a video recording of a blonde girl, stunning to look at but, alas for me, fully clothed.

"Well Tony, last week out lovely lass from Lancashire, Preston's finest Lisa-Jayne won an incredible £3,200. Since then she has had 27 proposals of marriage through the post. She's going to pick out the offer she likes best, and we at the Fantasy TV studios here, are paying for her and the very lucky winner to have an all expenses paid weekend break at a luxury hotel in the heart of lively London."

The smoothie Tony reached into his pocket and pulled out an envelope. He showed how hard he must brush his teeth before continuing, "Well, it should have been 28 proposals, but I forgot to post mine."

I didn't find him remotely funny, but the audience broke into hysterics. Perhaps they had something else written on their cue boards.

"So, Abigail," continued the compere, "what's our hunky fireman John been up to since he came on the show last week?"

A handsome rugged male in his early twenties appeared on screen surrounded by reporters. Abigail's voice-over reported.

"Well Tony, last week John won a staggering £5,700."

The audience let out an exaggerated "Ooooh!"

Abigail continued. "Since then a top Californian adult film company has offered our John a very lucrative contract to make twelve movies in sunny Santa Delicio. It seems that in America, at least, they're going to see an awful lot more of John."

Back came Tony Day.

"Well, good luck John. Looking at that fine figure of a

man is enough to turn me gay," he exuded. This only confirmed my suspicions about the compere's sexuality.

"So who have we got on tonight's show for all the lucky lads and lasses?" he continued.

Back came the voice of Terry. "Well, tonight is a senior citizens special. We have two very special contestants – 87 year-old Ada from Walthamstow and 79 year-old Albert from Liverpool. They are both ready, willing and able to play 'Truth or Bare'. In fact, at this afternoon's dress rehearsal, they were both so keen it was all that we could do to stop them taking their clothes off."

Tony interrupted. "Not so much a dress rehearsal then, more like an undress rehearsal."

Once again the audience burst out laughing.

Terry continued: "Ada knows that if she gets the questions right it's money in the bank, but if she's wrong then of course it's corsets that she'll lose. She told me before the show that she's not gone all the way since 1946. Let's see if she'll go all the way tonight – all the way to our golden jackpot of £25,000.

Abigail's voice-over came back on with some sort of patter about Albert and his dentures, but mentally I'd already switched off. This was a double blow to my lechery. The National Union of Disciples of Eden had arranged a number of attractive lady streakers at sports events up and down the country. But Fish Park, illustrious home of Grimchester United, had not been blessed by a visit from Bazooka Brenda or any of the other stripping lovelies, any more than my television screen was going to be blessed by them tonight.

A wrinkled Albert had appeared on the screen looking like a spruced up Steptoe Senior.

"You know," said Penny thoughtfully, "I think I was wrong earlier. Do you remember when we went to the Black Forest and accidentally came across that group of nudists in the forest?"

"Yes."

"Well, I'm not prudish, quite the opposite, but do you remember those Germans? They were huge, awful mounds of fat. I quite like the human body if it's someone sun-burned, young and attractive. But have you noticed how it's always middle-aged people with bodies past their sell-by date that want to show off all their bits that would be better left covered up?"

"Yes."

Penny looked at the wrinkled face of Albert. Compere Tony had to keep knocking Albert's hands away as he kept on trying to take off his shirt, accompanied by howls of laughter from an audience on nitrous oxide overkill.

"Yes, I think that I was wrong earlier," she concluded. "Perhaps it's not such a good idea to have that conference in Mudiford after all."

Part Three:

WHAT GOES UP…

EPILOGUE

THE FINAL CHAPTER

It had been a very good meeting of the planning committee. For once I had been at my eloquent best, speaking persuasively on a couple of items that I had finally managed to bring forward to the agenda, and receiving generally warm support from the other members.

The first was that details of all planning applications should be displayed at Mudiford Public Library and other sites throughout the district. Additionally, a copy of the plans would be available in every town and village for members of the general public to see. Suitable guardian-volunteers had already been found almost everywhere. I would myself be looking after those for Oakleigh. Hopefully this would reduce the chance assassination of a noted tree, or suchlike, slipping through by stealth.

The second success was to obtain a grant towards a local tree census that a national environmental group wanted to carry out. It was only £250, but, more importantly, it showed the council's support for the aims of the project.

The Conservatives, who held a large majority on the committee had obviously not been told how to vote on either issue. They listened attentively, couldn't see any devious hidden agenda to the idea, and most of them put their hands up to support the motions.

The short drive back from the District Council offices in Mudiford had been even more leisurely than usual in the face of driving wind and rain, so I had missed the main evening news by the time I arrived home. After a cursory greeting peck to Penny, I settled down in my favourite armchair, next to the gas fire, to watch the local news.

The first couple of items were of little interest, and as the third was introduced it looked likely to be the same.

"The region has today been battered by some of the worst storms this year, with power lines down at Little Ilkley, and the Rivers Erb and Mere put on flood alert. The rain and high winds have had a particularly devastating affect on one village. David Golstaff reports from the village of Oakleigh."

The scene switched from the studio to David Golstaff holding a microphone whilst battling with the wind and rain. There, on the television screen in my living room was a half-recognised scene of destruction in the background, and I sat bolt upright as the reporter spoke.

"As you can see, it's still wet and windy here. Earlier this evening the storms brought down an old tree here, and in the process a number of recently-built homes were damaged. With me here is Robin Tranter, whose house has suffered the worst damage. Thank you for joining us, Robin, can you tell us exactly what happened?"

"Well yes. There was a lot of wind here. You know, like now. This is only a small estate, you know. Expensive executive homes. Anyway, in the middle of the estate was some rotten old tree. Supposed to be historic or something. When the estate was built, you know, the council went and left the tree in the middle of all of the houses. Well, you know, with all this wind today. It blew down, didn't it. I don't know what the council was playing at... you know, leaving a rotten old tree like that. It was lucky it didn't kill someone. When it blew down."

Oops!

"So are many houses damaged?" asked the reporter, as he battled to hold his microphone.

"At least five. Mine's the worst, you know. The main window at the front is smashed, the roof is badly damaged and I reckon my BMW will be written off. One of the main branches went straight through the sun-roof, you know."

"So what are you going to do about it? Sue the council?"

"Too right. What I want to know is what our local councillor was doing. You know, letting the council leave the tree there in the first place. Yes we're all going to sue the council."

"Thank you for speaking to us." The reporter turned to face the camera full on. "This is David Golstaff reporting for West Anglia News here at King Henry's Oak Estate in Oakleigh."

The calamity was too much. I switched off the television.

Oh well, I suppose that there's always next year to improve the village – and to change the world.